The Spaces Between Us

The Spaces Between Us

A Story of Neuroscience, Evolution, and Human Nature

MICHAEL S. A. GRAZIANO

OXFORD
UNIVERSITY PRESS

Oxford University Press is a department of the University of Oxford. It furthers the University's objective of excellence in research, scholarship, and education by publishing worldwide. Oxford is a registered trade mark of Oxford University Press in the UK and certain other countries.

Published in the United States of America by Oxford University Press
198 Madison Avenue, New York, NY 10016, United States of America.

Library of Congress Cataloging-in-Publication Data
Names: Graziano, Michael S. A., 1967– author.
Title: The spaces between us : a story of neuroscience, evolution, and human nature / Michael S. A. Graziano.
Description: New York, NY : Oxford University Press, [2018]
Identifiers: LCCN 2017004294 (print) | LCCN 2017024720 (ebook) |
ISBN 9780190461027 (UPDF) | ISBN 9780190461034 (EPUB) |
ISBN 9780190461010 (hardback)
Subjects: LCSH: Cognitive neuroscience. | Brain. | Consciousness. |
Personal space. | BISAC: PSYCHOLOGY / Cognitive Psychology.
Classification: LCC QP360.5 (ebook) | LCC QP360.5 .G73 2018 (print) |
DDC 612.8/233—dc23
LC record available at https://lccn.loc.gov/2017004294

9 8 7 6 5 4 3 2 1

Printed by Sheridan Books, Inc., United States of America

This book is for the Gross lab, where so many of us grew up.

Contents

A Note on Terminology

Peripersonal neurons are cells in the brain that monitor the space around the body. Their activity rises like a Geiger counter to indicate the location of objects entering a margin of safety. The neurons can detect an intruding object through vision, hearing, touch, and even by the memory of where objects are positioned in the dark.

In the psychology literature of the 1960s, *personal space* referred to a social safety buffer around the body that varied in size depending on anxiety, status, and other factors.

In the past few years, researchers have begun to realize just how deep the connection runs between the personal space of psychology and the peripersonal neurons of the brain, and just how connected they are to our everyday behavior.

The Spaces Between Us

Chapter 1

The Second Skin

WE ALL HAVE AN INVISIBLE, PROTECTIVE BUBBLE around us. Personal space, margin of safety, bad breath zone, duck-and-flinch buffer—whatever you call it, we have it constantly switched on like a force field. It comes in layers, some layers close to the skin like a bodysuit, others farther away like a quarantine tent. Elaborate networks in the brain monitor those protective bubbles and keep them clear of danger by subtly, or sometimes drastically, adjusting our actions. You walk through a cluttered room weaving effortlessly around the furniture. A pigeon swoops past your head in the street and you duck. You stand a little farther from your boss than from your friend, and much closer to your lover. Usually hidden under the surface of consciousness, occasionally rising into awareness, personal space affects every part of human experience.

In this book I tell the story of personal space. The story extends from initial observations made almost a hundred years ago to the most recent, ongoing experiments in neuroscience. In the first part of the book I describe how scientists in the early twentieth century made a series of observations about zebras, birds, Frenchmen, Americans, and other fascinating animals. Their investigations were often colorful, sometimes a little horrifying, but led to foundational ideas about how we organize the spaces around our bodies.

Then I describe how neuroscientists (including myself) uncovered an astonishing and elegant mechanism in the brain that monitors personal space and coordinates the actions that steer us clear of danger. The neuroscience of personal space is one of the most beautiful and simple stories in brain science, and also now one of the best understood.

The remaining chapters describe the most recent insights into how our invisible second skin impacts almost every aspect of our lives. We wrap our personal space around handheld tools such as forks or golf clubs. Nobody would ever pass a driving test if we couldn't extend our margin of safety around the edges of the car. The way people stand near each other at a party is determined by the unconscious rules of personal space. A model poses in a fashion magazine with her head tilted and her long neck revealed, as if at a primal level she's saying, "I'm exposing my carotid artery. See how far I've dropped my defensive shield for you?" Even a smile may have originally evolved from a simple defensive cringe that says, "You're bigger than me and I'm definitely not a threat!" In these and many other ways, the hidden story of personal space connects specific mechanisms in the brain with the psychology of everyday events, our social behavior, and the evolution of our most human characteristics, such as facial expressions and tool use.

The final chapter of this book tells a personal story. When that invisible second skin breaks down, the results can be devastating, rippling outward into all aspects of life. I saw it first-hand in my son, who was born with subtle inconsistencies in his ability to process space and coordinate movement. What seemed like a minor setback, surely easy to overcome with physical therapy, spun out of control, and his elementary school experience came crashing down on him. With a disrupted personal space you cannot properly interface with the rest of the world. Sitting at a desk, holding a pencil, playing tag with a group of kids, judging the right interpersonal distances in the classroom—all of these ordinary abilities were disrupted. His teachers were so disturbed by a feeling of strangeness about his behavior that they rejected him and actually tried to kick him out of school. We had to go to court to show that he had a disability and that it could be helped by specific interventions.

Although I had studied personal space for years, I didn't understand it until I encountered it in that frightening personal context.

It isn't a scientific abstraction. It's real, and it infiltrates almost all aspects of our lives.

This book is meant for anyone interested—whether you're a student, a parent, a scientist, or any philosopher of life. The science is explained as clearly as I know how to do so, assuming no specialized background knowledge. I wanted to write a story that anyone would be interested in reading. At the same time, I did not simplify. In any scientific story, the quirks and complications are often the most interesting parts, if they can be presented clearly. Therefore, I hope this book is just as valuable to my colleagues in neuroscience as to anyone else. My goal in writing this book was to convey the richness and relevance of an astonishing, ongoing area of scientific research that is not as well known to the public as it should be.

Chapter 2

A Startling Discovery

I MAGINE IT'S THE 1920S AND YOU'RE A WORLD WAR I VETERAN in a German psychiatric hospital. You're suffering from shell shock, as it's called at the time. You're led to an examination room where Dr. Hans Strauss[1] is waiting for you. He greets you in a friendly, reassuring manner. His assistant, operating a hand-crank movie camera, records the encounter. You have no idea why anyone would film this exam. No one has explained the visit to you. As you stand in front of the charming Dr. Strauss, a hidden, second assistant creeps up silently behind you, holds a handgun just behind your head, aims it at the ceiling, and fires a shot. Your extreme reaction is recorded on film, and Dr. Strauss has his data. Thank you for your participation. You may go now.

Sometimes the surprised participants are hospitalized veterans, sometimes patients with other psychiatric issues, some have movement disorders, some are normal people off the street—men, women, even children. Whoever they are, Dr. Strauss is interested in their initial reaction to the gunshot, the acoustic startle. It happens within a fraction of a second—so fast that until these experiments nobody knew its properties. It's obvious that we tend to jump at a loud sound, maybe scream, spin around to take a look, but all those responses are slow. There's a much faster, more basic, more primitive response built into simple circuits in the brainstem.

The startle is not an emotional response. It happens before the emotions can kick in. It's so fast, the victims sometimes report the spooky impression of ducking down a fraction of a second *before* the sound. They don't actually have a Jedi-like ability to predict danger a moment into the future. This weird backward impression arises because the reflex is triggered before any of the slower, higher processing systems in the brain can register the sound. Human perception lags behind reality by at least a tenth of a second, probably more, whereas the startle reflex is ten times faster than that.

The reflex varies in strength from patient to patient, sometimes barely a flutter, sometimes a whopping big reaction, but the general shape of the response is astonishingly consistent. Dr. Strauss calls it "das Zusammenschrecken."[1] The German word, roughly translated as a "whole-body shrinking," is actually a good description of the act. The patient shrinks down, spine curved forward, knees bent, chin down and shoulders raised, hands pulled across the front, face contracted into a mighty squint that puckers the skin around the eyes and exposes the teeth.

Every part of it is designed for efficient protection. It's the first line of defense before the brain can compute anything specific about the threat. Why wait the extra milliseconds until the circuitry figures out where the threat comes from, what type of object is attacking you, or whether the event is a false alarm? In the first fraction of a second the startle reflex puts you into a generalized safety stance.

Statistically speaking, carnivores go for the throat. Therefore, a useful part of the reflex is pulling the head down and raising the shoulders. Crouching makes you a smaller target for any attack. Pulling your arms over your abdomen protects both your soft belly and your vulnerable hands. But the fastest and most consistent part of the reflex is the facial contraction. The muscles in the face spasm in just the right way to close the lids and pucker the skin around the eyes into a protective cushion. These are the most fundamental protective actions built into the basement of the brain.

To our modern sensibilities, Dr. Strauss's experiments have a breathtaking brutality. You wonder what happened to the people in those studies. Did he think his treatment was quite the right intervention for post-traumatic stress disorder? Did it improve doctor–patient trust? Did he think that a bonbon would make everything okay for the little girl after a gun went off behind her head? If nothing else, in today's world he'd be sued for the hearing damage. His experiment was typical of an earlier age that was innocent of ethics committees—direct, informative, and probably should never have been done. But it did lay a scientific foundation. It began the study of how the brain maintains a safety buffer around the body.

In the 1930s two American researchers, Carney Landis and William Hunt, carried on the scientific investigation of the startle reflex.[2] They repeated the pistol shot experiment and confirmed Strauss's observations. They also tried a range of other stimuli on "fifteen female subjects" otherwise unspecified. They tried a jet of ice water between the shoulder blades, an electric shock to the hand, a pinprick to the thigh, a flashbulb, and a car horn. In each case the stimulus was unannounced. For example, the women were told to hold a piece of equipment and then unexpectedly given a shock through it. And when one person distracted the woman's attention, another one (maybe hiding under the table?) stuck her in the leg with a pin. I wonder if the experimenters did these studies on women for fear that men would punch them in the nose?

The startle pattern was sometimes present but less consistent following these many other stimuli than following the gunshot, maybe because the offending stimuli could not match the same sudden onset of a loud sound. A gunshot rises to maximum loudness almost instantaneously. At the same time, the auditory system in the brain processes information on the order of microseconds, much faster than any other sensory system. This may be why a starting pistol works so well at a race, as opposed to, say, a starting flashbulb or a starting needle goosing you.

The acoustic startle reflex is the most pure, stripped-down, primitive essence of self-protection. Other, more complex protective mechanisms in the brain are layered on top of the startle pathways, but these more complex mechanisms are harder to study. Because the startle reflex is so simple in its scientific concept and at the same time so rich in its details, it has become a popular object of study among psychologists and neuroscientists. It's a beautiful model system.

In the decades since Strauss's experiments, many of the details have been worked out in people, rats, cats (who have a pronounced startle response, as all cat owners know), and other animals.[1-5] The startle reflex runs through some of the most primitive pathways in the base of the brain. Information from the senses flows directly into a rich network of neurons located in the brainstem. That network goes by the jargonistic name of the "pontine reticular formation."[3-5] It has an ancient evolutionary pedigree, dating back possibly as far as half a billion years. The network probably has many functions, but at least one is to coordinate the startle response. The transmission line from sensory-in to movement-out is so direct that only a hundredth of a second passes between the onset of a loud sound and the rise of activity in the muscles around the eyes. It's a model of efficiency—and needs to be for our survival.

The best way to appreciate the startle reflex is to film it and watch the film frame by frame, the same as when Strauss studied it a century ago.[1] When my own lab began to study protective reflexes, in the early 2000s, the video cameras came out, and the lab became a dangerous place. Graduate students lurked in hidden corners and lunged out with a Velociraptor scream. I got hit with a wet wad of paper towel while somebody secretly filmed me. Sundry plastic bugs and a pair of taxidermized monkey arms found their way pretty much everywhere, especially inside the lunch refrigerator. I confess, I once took a cow eyeball from a dissection class, wrapped it in foil, and gave it to a colleague as a chocolate truffle. Alas, I never did film the moment of truth for the eyeball truffle, but I heard the scream from his office down the hall. To be honest, the motivation for these "experiments" wasn't always scientific curiosity. We were also just sophomoric. But sometimes scientists get so caught up in numbers and procedures that we forget to see the larger picture. For insight into the expressive range of the human face, nothing can beat watching a film of a colleague screaming his head off in slow motion.

When you look at still frames of a startle reaction, two features stand out most: the pursing of skin around the eyes and the flashing of teeth. The upper lip pulls up, baring the upper teeth, so that the face seems to flash a bit of white. It looks like a fleeting smile or a laugh.

A lot of guesses have been floated about the purpose of exposing the teeth during a startle reflex, mainly speculations about preparing to bite somebody. If you're about to be attacked, maybe it's good to unsheathe your teeth? But a close look at the movement, especially if you measure muscle activity in the face, suggests a different function. If you expose your teeth to bite a hamburger, you recruit a set of muscles that ring the mouth. In contrast, the startle reflex recruits muscles around the eyes and in the cheeks. The forehead is mobilized downward and the cheeks are mobilized upward, dragging the upper lip with them. As a consequence, the eyes are protected in wrinkles of muscle and skin.

You'll know exactly what I mean if you've ever walked from a dark indoor space into an ultra-bright, sun-saturated summer day. Your whole face contracts into a kind of sun smile, or maybe a sun grimace, exposing your upper teeth, bunching your cheeks upward, wrinkling the skin around your eyes and protecting them from the excess light. You're not preparing to bite anything. That pseudo-smile is a byproduct of protecting the eyes.

They say that the eyes are the windows to the soul. When you think about it though, the eyeballs themselves aren't really the windows. If you could look at a pair of eyeballs minus the rest of the face, you wouldn't learn much. I suppose you'd learn where the eyes are looking and how dilated the pupils are, information indicative of the person's state of mind. But the broadband on that information is limited. Really, for reading another person, everything surrounding the eyes matters most. The windows to the soul are the eyelids that can narrow skeptically or open wide, the eyebrows that move and shape expressively, the sly wrinkles at the outer corners or on the bridge of the nose, the upward bunching of the cheeks—the many tensions and relaxations rioting around the center.

Ask any professional portraitist (I know this from when I tried unsuccessfully to learn the art) and you will be told that, although the eyes are the most important part of the portrait, the eyeballs themselves are not so interesting to paint. They're merely bluish-white ovals with a black dot and a reflection. The emotional expression, and the challenge to the painter, lies in all the subtleties crowding around the eyeballs.

It may not be a coincidence that those windows to the soul correspond so exactly to the epicenter of the startle reflex. The startle has a side effect that has nothing to do with self-protection: it broadcasts personal information. The reason is that the startle reflex is strongly influenced by your internal emotional and attentional states. As fast and stripped down as the reflex may be, as much as it relies on primitive pathways through the base of the brain that evolved before any higher thought or emotion, it is nonetheless influenced by networks all throughout the brain. Mood, thought, attention, and expectation sift through cortical and subcortical circuitry, reach that pontine reticular formation, and affect the startle reflex.[3-10] The startle is in turn visible to anyone else watching.

For example, startle is affected by anxiety. One way to make people anxious in an experiment is to electrically shock them periodically. As you're cringing and waiting for the next shock, if you're blasted with an unexpected loud sound, your startle reflex to that sound is greatly exaggerated.[11]

Even if you're subjected to less extreme irritants to put you off your ease, like foul odors or unpleasant pictures, your startle reaction grows stronger.[12-14] People who suffer from anxiety disorders have a measurably enhanced startle reaction.[8-16] They really are more jumpy. Maybe that's why Strauss obtained such clear results from the psychiatric patients in his classic experiment.[1] He probably got a good reaction out of them.

The fact is, your startle reflex is susceptible to your inner moods and thoughts. And this susceptibility has a monumental consequence. It's one of those right-angle bends in evolution that makes biologists happy. Another creature, watching your startle reaction, could, in principle, learn a great deal about your inner state. Are you confident or anxious? Are you on your guard for a possible attack, or are you totally oblivious to the present risks? Are you dominant over the people around you, or do you feel frightened by them? Your reactions to the sound of a broken twig or the unexpected touch of a fly landing on the back of your neck—just how much you crouch, and especially how much of the startle reaction flits across your face, pops out in the wrinkles around your eyes, or shows in the rising movement of your upper lip as you flash some teeth—these reactions can convey crucial psychological information to anyone watching. An especially enterprising creature might even probe your startle reaction by looming at you or barking, for the specific purpose of extracting information.

The startle reflex, therefore, doesn't just protect your body. It leaks information about your inner state to the rest of the world. And startle behaviors are not subtle. They're often obvious. You might as well put a neon billboard on your head. You can't unplug that billboard, either. It isn't safe to kill the startle just to stop broad-casting your weaknesses.

Survival requires the startle, and the startle is an exploitable data breech.

Of course, the startle reflex is not, itself, a social gesture. It's not a smile, a laugh, or a frown. It's simply a reflex that evolved to protect the body, especially the eyes. But in its own primitive way, it does broadcast psychological information. In order for the startle reflex to spark an evolutionary explosion of new social signals, all you need is a creature with enough brain capacity to look at others, especially at their eyes, perceive the subtleties in tension and movement, and use the stolen information to decide how to act next.

The situation reminds me of a poker game. Poker players often have tells. For example, a player might unconsciously pick at his fin-gernails or scratch the bridge of his nose when he's nervous. A good player will notice the tell immediately and use it to advantage. It may not convey a lot of information, but it conveys enough to give the observer a statistical edge. On the other hand, a good player can also *mimic* tells, seeming to appear nervous or confident, sending inter-ference and thereby strategically influencing the behavior of his or her opponents. Give it a million years of evolution and who knows what elaborate, ritualized signals and countersignals might emerge in *Homo five-card*.

In later chapters I'll describe how some of our most common, ritualized emotional expressions, like smiling, laughing, and crying, might trace their evolutionary ancestry to basic defensive reflexes and their side effect of leaking psychological information.

Chapter 3

The Flight Zone of the Zebra

B EFORE HEINI HEDIGER, ZOOS WERE DEPRESSING PLACES. A cage was a bare concrete box with bars. After Hediger's visionary work as the director of the Zurich Zoo, from the 1950s to the 1970s, and after his careful studies of animal behavior,[1] zoo cages became elaborate environments shaped for the emotional needs of the animals. He is deservedly called the father of zoo biology.

He also launched the study of personal space. It's easy to see how Hediger might have been attuned to the protective spaces around animals. Zoo animals, after all, are comfortable only if their cages form a safe, protective bubble.

Hediger believed that psychologists, biologists, and, for that matter, poets were misled by romantic notions about animal behavior. Most of them assumed that love and appetite—sex and food—were the essential drives. Depending on whether you were an optimist or a cynic, either love made the world go round or greed did. To Hediger, however, the strongest drive was obvious: protecting the self from bodily harm. As he put it in his groundbreaking book on animal behavior, in 1955, "The satisfaction of hunger and sexual appetite can be postponed; not so escape from a dangerous enemy."[2] In other words, your first task is to keep yourself alive, because once you're dead the game is over. To Hediger, almost every moment of a wild animal's life was focused on the problem of immediate safety.

It was for this reason that animals were so attentive to the spaces around them.

Hediger observed animals in zoos, in the urban world around him, and in the wild, especially in Africa.[1] Based on those observations, he broke with the prevailing scientific tradition. In the 1950s, animal psychology was dominated by behaviorism. That scientific philosophy placed an almost total emphasis on stimulus and response. Animals were input–output devices, and science could not legitimately study the cognitive complexity in between. Hediger noticed, however, that something complex must be going on inside. Animals seemed to have an internal map of the spaces around them. For one thing, they had territories.

Hediger described a moment of insight when he was flying over a rural part of Europe.[1] He looked down to see cultivated fields laid out in abutting plots in a giant mosaic over the landscape. It came to him that people are like other animals in this respect, organizing the landscape into adjoining territories. Mice may have small territories measurable in meters, lions may have enormous ones measurable in kilometers, but the spatial pattern is similar across species.

A territory is hard to explain as stimulus–response behavior. It's more a spatial concept—something abstract inside the brain. The animal doesn't see the whole territory all at once. It lays claim to the area and then keeps track of it over long stretches of time.

More than just *having* territories, animals *partition* their territories. And this insight turned out to be particularly useful for zoo husbandry. An animal's territory has an internal arrangement that Hediger compared to the inside of a person's house. Most of us assign separate functions to separate rooms, but even if you look at a one-room house you will find the same internal specialization. In a cabin or a mud hut, or even a Mesolithic cave from 30,000 years ago, this part is for cooking, that part is for sleeping; this part is for making tools and weaving, that part is for waste. We keep a neat functional organization. To a varying extent, other animals do the same. A part of an animal's territory is for eating, a part for sleeping, a part for swimming or wallowing, a part may be set aside for waste, depending on the species of animal.

In the case of zebras, according to Hediger, a part of the territory is reserved for scratching itchy fur on termite mounds. In the African plains, termite mounds can grow to six-foot pillars of brown, knobbly stuff as hard as concrete. A zebra prefers to include at least one scratching post inside its territory. That part of the territory is used for that specific purpose. The zebra makes a well-worn track through the field directly to the scratching post. There the animal might be seen alternating between a cautious watchfulness and an ecstatic abandon as it rubs its head and neck. All around the termite mound, the ground is carpeted with coarse, short zebra hair.

After observing this behavior, Hediger immediately went back to his zoo and installed a concrete termite mound in the zebra enclosure. As soon as the zebras were let back in, they ran to the scratching post, threw themselves on it, and rubbed so hard that they knocked it to the ground in a few seconds. A new one had to be installed and bolted down.

Psychologists distinguish between at least two different ways that the brain processes space.[3–6] One way is to process the locations of objects with respect to external landmarks. This is sometimes called *environmental space* or *allocentric space*. For example, the chairs are around the table, the tree is next to the lake, the public library is on the east side of the city next to the laundromat.

A second way is to process the locations of objects with respect to your own body. This is sometimes called *egocentric space*. For example, my coffee cup is to my right, the lamp is to my left, the keyboard is near me, the door is farther from me.

An animal's territory is an example of allocentric space. It's space with respect to external landmarks. It stays fixed as the animal moves through it. But Hediger noticed that most animals construct a second kind of territory that is egocentric. It's a small, portable territory, a bubble of space that moves as you move, and it serves a specific function. He called it an *escape distance*, or a *flight zone*.

When a wildebeest sees a potentially dangerous animal—a lion, or perhaps Hediger with a tape measure walking around the veldt—it doesn't simply run. This isn't a simple stimulus–response proposition. The animal seems to make a geometric assessment. It remains calm until the threat enters a protected zone, an invisible bubble around itself, and then the wildebeest moves away and reinstates the flight zone. That escape distance is apparently consistent enough to measure it to the meter. I can imagine Hediger walking up to the same poor harassed animal over and over, interrupting its afternoon grazing, trying to get a reliability measure.

In general, the larger the animal, the larger the escape distance. According to Hediger, a wall lizard can be approached to within a few meters before it suddenly bolts. A crocodile has more like a fifty-meter flight distance. And yes, crocodiles generally move away as people approach, though presumably not always. The size of the flight zone adjusts depending on circumstances, such as appetite.

Hediger describes a poignant story about an adjustable flight zone.[1] The story involves a colleague of his, Dr. Greppin, the director of a Swiss nursing home. One of the doctor's less pleasant jobs was to periodically clear the sparrows from the grounds of the nursing home. At first, the sparrows had a flight zone of about thirty meters. After a few days of shotgun treatment, during which most of them were killed, the surviving sparrows had a flight zone of about one hundred fifty meters. It didn't protect them much from the gun, but their experiences had measurably changed their behavior.

And yet the flight zone is not the same thing as fear. It's also not the same thing as running or flying away. It's neither an emotion nor a behavior. It can certainly come with those properties, but the flight zone is a specific spatial computation that can proceed in the animal's head in the absence of any obvious fear or escape.

I saw a particularly clear example once, back when I worked with primates. A little girl monkey was in a large enclosure filled with climbers and toys that we had collected for her enjoyment. She used to exercise in that enclosure a few hours a day, and I would sometimes sit quietly in a corner and watch just for the pleasure of seeing an excited and playful simian. She would bounce around the place like a gas molecule. On one occasion, as I was watching, I began to notice something peculiar. The pattern was so subtle that I had to collect data in a notebook to see it. Her movements seemed random, jumping to whatever caught her fancy, but when averaged over time, they formed a kind of a doughnut. She simply never went into a specific part of the enclosure. Right at the center of that taboo zone was a stuffed toy monkey that we had put in for her amusement. It obviously didn't amuse her. She didn't scream at it, face it, grimace at it, cringe away from it, show any fear or any anxiety. She didn't show any overt reaction at all. But her ongoing behavior was profoundly shaped by it. She knew it was there and kept a specific distance from it, as if it were ringed by a magic circle. Of course, the magic circle was actually around *her*. It was her safety buffer with respect to a freaky monkey with button eyes.

Animals have a safety buffer with respect to threatening objects, predators, and even other individuals of the same species. One of Hediger's most famous photographs[1] was of a line of seagulls sitting on a log, spaced in such perfectly even increments that they looked almost like carved decorations. The gulls had a natural avoidance distance with respect to each other, a personal distance. Since they weren't in danger of attack from each other, the distance was only about half a meter. Nonetheless, they had constructed a spatial zone around their bodies that was kept clear of other birds.

When Hediger visited the natural history museum in London, he noticed a mistake in a diorama. Two stuffed birds were sitting on a wire. They were so close that their wing feathers touched. Such a reduced personal spacing might be appropriate for some species, but not others. As he put it, "This sort of thing only happens to stuffed swallows, never to living ones."[7] He told the museum curator, who had the two misbehaving birds separated.

According to Hediger, the flight zone shrinks with domestication. He proposed that domestication *is* the process of losing the flight zone. The difference between a wild species and a domesticated one, in that view, lies in a single number computed in the animal's brain, a safety distance—simple, measurable, scientific.

I think Hediger went too far on that point. There's a wonderful and growing literature on the genetic, physical, and social differences between wild and domestic animals,[8-10] and the flight zone is only one of many metrics that change. Besides, domestic animals do have at least some flight zone left over. Any farmer, or, for that matter, any good herd dog, knows about the escape zones around an animal.[11] If you stand in a specific place with respect to a cow, or a dog stands at that place, the cow will shy away in a predictable manner. By manipulating these so-called pressure points around the animal, you can herd it effectively. Good herding is not about running at an animal or yapping at its heels. It's about positioning yourself at the crucial points in the animal's space. (I know this first-hand because, when I was younger, our neighbor's cows often escaped onto our property and we had to herd them back home.)

As a zoologist and lover of nature, Hediger's sympathies were firmly on the side of the wild animals. He was primed to think of domestication as a dismantling of the natural state, and of humans as the enemy of all nature. Maybe this explains the blind spot in his understanding of human behavior. He claimed that people had domesticated themselves to the point where they had no flight zone left whatsoever. They may have a chatty social space around them, but not the same cautious, protective space of the wild animal. As he rather dramatically put it, "Man is moreover the only creature able to free himself from the elementary function of escape. By this self-release, man clearly stands apart from the rest of creation, and, as the arch enemy, is the focus of all animal escape reactions."[12]

For all of Hediger's brilliant observations and contributions, he got this one item wrong. People do have an escape zone—not just a social space into which we invite other people, but a robust margin of safety from which we exclude each other—and it is one of the dominant influences on us. It helped to shape human nature.

The next chapter describes how psychologists transferred Hediger's insights about the flight zone from wild animals directly to the human experience and opened up an entirely new way to understand our social world.

Chapter 4

The French Stare
Too Much, and My Lover
Has a Bulgy Nose

E DWARD HALL WAS A PRODUCT OF A MORE RACIST AND
  sexist world.

In his 1966 book, *The Hidden Dimension*,[1] Hall describes an unpleasant encounter he had in a hotel lobby. He was sitting in an isolated chair, hoping to be left in peace while waiting for a friend to arrive. In the meantime, a stranger walked up and stood so close to him that Hall could have touched the guy. He could hear the man breathing and could even smell him. As Hall put it, "If the lobby had been crowded with people, I would have understood his behavior, but in the empty lobby his presence made me exceedingly uncomfortable."[2] Every time Hall squirmed or glared, to try to send a message, the man merely edged closer. It was outrageous. Finally, a group of people arrived and the intruder left Hall's chair to join them. By their language, Hall realized that the people were Arabic. Well sure, Hall thought to himself, that explains it.

In Hall's interpretation, Arabs have a culturally different take on personal space. They prefer to stand close enough to be within smell distance—body smell and breath smell. They consider it rude to turn away and avoid breathing onto another person's face because that would be denying the person your living warmth. Moreover, if an Arab wants the spot you've chosen, such as a comfortable chair in a hotel lobby, he won't leave the place to you—a finders-keepers attitude more typical of Americans. Instead, the Arab will mooch in on you, crowding you in hopes you'll cede the ground to him. As Hall became visibly agitated, the Arab man noticed and moved ever closer, presumably hopeful that he was about to drive away the competition and win the chair for himself.

I remain skeptical of the details. Hall's case is built on the worst sort of stereotypes and anecdotes that trigger my science warning beeper. And yet, leaving aside the details, he gets at a deep truth about human behavior, something that he called "proxemics." He borrowed the insights that Hediger had just published about wild animals and transferred them to human behavior.

In Hall's formulation, human experience is organized by space. Public squares, lawns, the arrangement of furniture in a room, greeting distances, lovers' embraces—all of these parts of our lives are built on the foundation of spatial perception. We arrange the space around us unconsciously but systematically. Some of our spatial preferences are universal and others are culturally specific. Hall's cultural observations are among the most interesting and also the most cringe-inducing. He discusses the Germans, the English, the French, Japanese, and Arabs, all in comparison to Americans. In the twenty-first century this overt comparison, especially without any actual data to back it up, would be so politically insensitive that it would never be published in the first place.

According to Hall, the Germans close their office doors to keep the integrity of a private space, whereas Americans consider a closed office door to be a sign of a secret meeting—or a sign of unfriendliness. An American businessman trying to work in Germany doesn't understand why everyone keeps walking into his office freely, as if they owned it. The reason is that he's left his door open, and nobody else understands the open door as a privacy barrier. To them it looks like the American is lonely and asking for company.

The French look directly at you, giving the impression of intruding on your space, even from a distance. This can cause confusion, especially in American women. According to Hall, American women who spend a few weeks in France will develop a fondness for the open stare, and when they return home they will feel ignored by American men.

The English grow up in crowded boarding schools with no private spaces, and as a result they develop a special way of seeking privacy—not by retreating to another room and relying on walls to protect their alone time, but by shutting themselves off with closed body language. They learn to recognize and respect this body language in others. Americans find it puzzling and stiff, sometimes to the point of rudeness. When a Brit and an American are in the same room, the American is always trying to break the silence and keep the conversation going, while the Brit is baffled about how to discourage this obtrusively friendly American assault.

The Japanese are a crowded people who depend on body-to-body contact to feel togetherness. As one Japanese priest put it to Hall, "It's when your hands touch and you feel the warmth of their bodies and everyone feels together—that's when you get to know the Japanese."[3]

I don't want to delve too deeply into Hall's cultural speculations. They're fascinating, worth reading, and probably have some validity, but the hairs stand on the back of my neck from the blatant stereotyping and casual observation. Without collecting data, without actually measuring behavior in an unbiased manner and doing a statistical comparison between cultures, I would prefer to be more cautious. But undeniably, Hall put his finger on something important in human experience. Maybe that's partly why I squirm when I read about it.

Hall divided the space around people into four zones of different sizes: intimate distance, personal distance, social distance, and public distance.[1]

Intimate distance is so close that you can't even focus your eyes properly. Hall paints the romantic appearance we present to a lover: "The nose is seen as over large and may look distorted, as will other features such as the lips, teeth, and tongue."[4] That about captures it.

Personal distance, standing just within arm's length, is more typical of a friendly conversation at a cocktail party or leaning in across a small coffee table.

Social distance, just beyond arm's length, is appropriate for a business meeting or a casual acquaintance.

Public distance is larger still. It can be many body-lengths, and voices must be raised to be heard.

Important public figures such as presidents have about a thirty-foot margin around them, a zone of respectful distance into which people do not venture unless specifically invited. At least that was Hall's interpretation. He gives a vivid description of the respectful zone around President Kennedy. Kennedy was a popular and charismatic president surrounded by friends and flatterers, but he seemed always to stand at the center of an empty circle about thirty feet in radius. I think our culture must have shifted since then. I have an equally vivid mental image of Governor Brewer sticking her finger aggressively into the face of President Obama in 2012—although by many accounts that incident may have stemmed from a different, racial dynamic.

After Hall published his observations in the 1960s, psychologists conducted a vast number of follow-up experiments to study the phenomenon of personal space and lift it out of the realm of casual impression.[5-43]

In many experiments, volunteers were asked to walk toward each other and stop when the interpersonal distance began to feel uncomfortable.[5-7] The volunteers knew they were being watched and measured and that self-consciousness might have affected their choices. Since the dance of personal space normally proceeds under the surface of consciousness, many scientists resorted to more covert procedures. For example, in one study, the experimenter walked up to random people in a public setting and stood or sat at a specific distance, often inappropriately close, and waited to see if the victim would remain or step away.[8] Many researchers passively observed how people behaved spontaneously in public, for example, surveilling a library and observing how people arranged themselves in chairs around a reading table. In one creepy study, men were observed in the restroom.[9] The idea was that, as a man's anxiety increases, he takes longer to start urinating, and the urination onset time should depend on whether other men are standing close or far away.

The most consistent finding out of this vast literature, the one fundamental result, is that personal space expands with anxiety. If you score high on stress, or if the experimenter stresses you ahead of time—maybe you take a test and are told that you failed it—your personal space grows with respect to other people.[5,7,10–16] If you're put at your ease, or the experimenter flatters your self-esteem ahead of time, your personal space shrinks.[17] In at least some studies, women have an especially large personal space when approached by men.[5,6,8,18–20] People in positions of social status or authority have a reduced personal space, especially toward each other.[21] A large man with an excess of self-confidence and who has just been flattered by admirers, Donald Trump, let's say, has the smallest personal buffer zone of all. And if he walks toward you while looking directly at you, your personal space may grow particularly large.

At first, the pattern seems to contradict the earlier observations. Both Hediger and Hall noted that dominant status came with a larger personal space. Hall pointed to the unspoken thirty-foot rule around President Kennedy.[1] Yet the data show that dominant individuals often have the *smallest* personal space. Which is right? It's easy to get that relationship wrong if you don't look closely and pick it apart. If a person such as a highly respected president has a clearing around him of thirty feet, it may look like a giant personal bubble of space centered on his body. But it's not *his* personal space. It's everyone else's personal space. Everyone else in the room has an expanded, thirty-foot nervous distance with respect to the alpha male, and the collective result is a kind of magic ring around the president. As he walks forward, people tend to clear out of the way.

When tested at finer precision, personal space tends to stick out farther in front than at the sides or behind.[18] When people are crowded together on the subway and the balloon of personal space is compressed, you can see its intrinsic shape particularly well. If you could sneak around with a tape measure and record the average distance between the body parts of adjacent travelers, you would see an overall trend toward buffering the front of the face and especially the eyes. As always, the eyes are the epicenter of self-protection.

And just to note: when tested carefully, Arabs and Americans are not significantly different in the size of their personal space, except for Arabic women, who may have a trend toward an expanded personal space when confronted by men who are not family.[22]

The main lesson from these experiments and observations is that personal space is protective. It's the region in which you *don't* want other people. It's not really a region into which you invite other people.

This modern account of personal space is quite different from the way Hediger or Hall first described it. Both of them thought that personal space and protective space were two different phenomena. In their formulation, humans didn't even have a protective flight zone. Instead, personal space was supposed to be a zone of invitation, almost like a sitting room, something arranged for the purpose of accepting in friends and organizing the conversation. The more comfortable and socially dominant you are, the larger that virtual welcoming room around you.

But the evidence points to a different pattern. Whether we're talking about a flight zone that extends a hundred meters from the body, a public distance that extends ten meters, or an intimate distance within a few centimeters, these spaces around the body are primarily protective. They are the zones in which you'd rather *not* have the other person. That margin of safety can shrink a hundred-fold toward the people you know and trust, but even a friend shouldn't get *too* close to your skin or you'll step back. Only during a few special behaviors, such as pair bonding and sex, do people shrink their personal space to nothing, out of mechanical necessity. Personal space is all about the zone where you keep people out, not the zone where you invite people in. It's an adjustable protective buffer.

By the 1980s, the psychological work on personal space had mainly died down. The phenomenon had been demonstrated in wild animals, zoo animals, and humans. Its basic properties had been measured and nobody seemed to know what to do with it next. That corner of the literature had reached an apparent saturation.

Then the neuronal underpinnings began to be discovered. At the start of my career as a scientist, in 1987, I found myself swept up in that surge of new research. We were uncovering beautiful and simple mechanisms in the brain—neurons that monitor bubbles of space around the body in intelligent and flexible ways, and that adjust ongoing behavior to keep the body safe.

The next chapter describes an accidental discovery I made as an undergraduate in a neuroscience lab, and how it diverted me into that area of research. At the time, I had no idea of its importance. I thought it would make a summer project, but instead it led to decades of research into how the brain reconstructs the world around us.

Chapter 5

Monkey Versus Ping-Pong Ball

A NIMAL EXPERIMENTATION IS A CHARGED TOPIC. SOME
scientists avoid any public presentation of their work, but
I don't follow that secretive approach. I'd rather share the incredible
truths that we learned about brain function.

And yet I can say very little here that speaks to the modern debate
about animals in research. I've been out of that loop for too long.
The regulations and standards are constantly changing and would
be unrecognizable to me now. For example, a lot of what we used to
do on our own twenty years ago is now done by a fleet of vets and
professional caretakers. That change is good, I think. In these respects
you will have to treat the next few chapters as a story of the past and
not a window into the present.

I spent eighteen years studying the neural mechanisms of personal space in monkeys. About ten years ago, when I ended my animal program in order to focus my scientific questions on a different
and more available primate (humans), I shipped my monkeys to a
sanctuary in Texas. There they still live in a large social group, in an
outdoor enclosure with an indoor attachment for inclement weather,
overseen by an attending vet. I fondly imagine them on hammocks
sipping banana daiquiris and reading *Tarzan of the Apes,* although
that's admittedly improbable.

To do animal research, or any kind of research for that matter, I think you need a strong belief in its importance. You need a larger vision and you need a lot of patience for the slow pace of experimental science. I'm a staunch believer in basic neuroscience research—it builds the vast, growing scaffold of knowledge about the brain on which all practical advances will ultimately depend. And personal space, as I will argue throughout this book, is one of the most crucial topics to study. It's mostly hidden under the surface of awareness, easy to ignore, and yet affects all aspects of our lives. It's foundational to almost all our behavior, and it wreaks havoc when it goes wrong developmentally in children or when it becomes disrupted in adults who suffer brain damage. I know all too well about its everyday importance through the experiences of my son, who was born with disturbances in personal space (as I'll describe in the last chapter of this book). The more of the mechanistic details that we can figure out, the better.

In the next five chapters I'll describe some of those mechanistic details, the systems in the brain that monitor the spaces around us and reflexively shape our behavior to keep us safe. These chapters delve into the neuroscience, the nuts and bolts of experiments, but they are more than just descriptions of data. I want to write about what it was like to stand at the center of scientific chaos and see the pieces gradually come together, one finding at a time. This is a story of discovery. For that reason, as I am acutely aware, my account is slanted toward my own experience. Although many other scientists contributed key experiments, the following chapters emphasize the work in my own lab, and I apologize for that self-centeredness.

When I was nineteen years old, a skinny and idealistic undergrad at Princeton University with big floppy hair, I joined a science lab to study the brain. It was 1987. The lab was run by Dr. Charles Gross, a sixties-looking dude with a tie-dye T-shirt and a shaggy, graying forest of hair and beard. I didn't know it at the time, but Charlie was probably the most successful neuroscience mentor of the twentieth century. More scientific movers and shakers came out of his lab than any other. It was sheer good luck for me that my path crossed with his.

We studied macaque monkeys. They're Old World monkeys found across Africa and Asia, small animals no more than knee-high, with brown fur, long tails, and dog-like snouts. They're intensely visual creatures able to recognize individual monkeys and people, able to react to the nuances of facial expression, but not very good in the auditory domain. They never did learn the sound of their own names. Sometimes people would ask me if these are the monkeys that learn sign language. No, they're not chimps. They're nowhere near as smart as that or as closely related to humans.

The first time I walked into the lab, I was led through a maze of corridors to the main experiment room and saw a monkey anesthetized and lying peacefully on a table. People in lab coats were crowded around the table, talking excitedly, projecting pictures on a screen in front of the animal. It was a bizarre scene for a newcomer.

At the time, the lab used a method that's now rare but for decades was a mainstay of neuroscience. It's called the *anesthetized prep*. I'll explain it in some detail here because it was the scientific heart of the lab. It was based on procedures used in human neurosurgery and involved anesthetizing a monkey under a surgical-grade, gaseous anesthesia so that the monkey felt nothing and was as comfortable as possible.

Through a surgical port on the head, a hair-thin tungsten wire was lowered by precision machinery, micron by micron, with exquisite delicacy into the anesthetized brain. The wire was insulated with varnish except at the tip, where the tiny cone of exposed metal could pick up faint electrical signals. The electrode was lowered into position next to a single nerve cell among the billions in the monkey's brain, picking up that neuron's signals and piping those tiny electrical pops and clicks to a loud speaker. To hear those clicks for the first time, when I first joined the lab, seemed close to a miracle. We were listening to the muttering of a single cell in that monkey's brain. (One of the more startling moments occurred when the electrode began to pick up the CB radio signals from a trucker on Route 1, and the neuron suddenly broke into a string of lurid profanity.)

We knew when the tip of the electrode was approaching a neuron because the pops and clicks would grow louder, and we knew when we went too far because the signals would begin to fade again into the background noise. If we kept lowering the electrode, the clicking of another cell would emerge out of the noise. We spent a lot of time adjusting the depth of the electrode, trying to position it perfectly next to a brain cell, listening to the sound like neuron-connoisseurs and watching squiggly green lines on an oscilloscope.

A living brain is never entirely silent. Even though the monkey was anesthetized, signals wandered around at a low level and much could be learned from that activity. When we had parked the electrode next to a neuron, that particular cell might give off an electrical click once every few seconds in a random rattle. If we found the right trigger to activate that part of the brain, suddenly the neuron would fire off a burst that sounded like a machine gun.

The task was to isolate a neuron in the brain, listen to its clicking, and figure out exactly what aspect of the world tickled it. The animal's eyes were covered in contact lenses and focused on a projection screen, and we'd shine images on the screen with a handheld projector. Did the neuron respond to a spot of light here, in the upper right corner, or there, a little lower down? Did it respond preferentially to a specific color? To a line tilted at a specific orientation? A specific complex shape? The neurons seemed to pick the world apart into features, each neuron tuned to a different feature, and it was up to us to figure out those triggers. By listening in on the smallest logic gates in the brain, we could begin to understand how the brain processed information and we could construct a map of which brain areas did what.

The experiments had a bizarre, drug-trippy quality. In the middle of the night, in the dead silence, when we were in that dark bunker of a room for too long and trace amounts of the gas anesthesia had begun to leak into the room air and mess with our brains, my imagination would play tricks on me. I'd see the monkey lift his arms slowly off the table in a vampire gesture and loom toward me. Once I even thought I saw the monkey dancing. I'd take a sharp look again, and the monkey would be as still as before, sleeping peacefully, his chest moving evenly up and down. That's as close as I ever came in my life to a drug high.

I think it's fair to say that Charlie Gross began social neuroscience, in the 1960s, with the discovery of face cells, neurons high up in the hierarchy of visual processing that are tuned to the sight of faces.[1] Show a face to a monkey, any face, whether a monkey or human face, or, for that matter, a cartoon face, and the face cells fire off a volley of activity as if they're shouting, "Hey! There's a face! Socially important!" The discovery of face cells proved that social processing was a specialized capability that had its own dedicated machinery in the brain. Social neuroscience began at that moment.

By the time I reached the lab, in 1987, face cells were long established. I wanted to branch into something different. I was young and brash and wanted to jump into the unknown, so I picked the most obscure corner of the brain that I knew about from my neuro-anatomy class and petitioned Charlie to let me study it. The claustrum is a thin sheet of neurons buried under the cerebral cortex, more or less just above the ears. (It's shown in Figure 5.1.) The claustrum is widely connected to the rest of the cortex, but nobody knows its function.[2]

Charlie gave the go-ahead and we began our experiment with the help of another researcher in the lab, Hillary Rodman. This experiment was a good early lesson to me in how science works. Everything you believe turns out to be wrong. Nothing goes as expected. And you need to keep your eyes open because interesting discoveries are

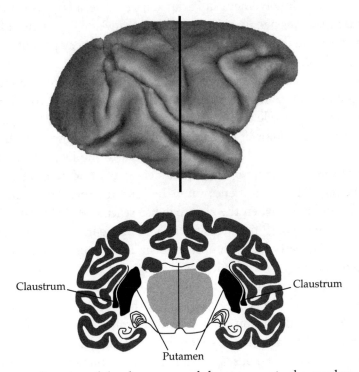

FIGURE 5.1 Location of the claustrum and the putamen in the monkey brain. **Top:** Image of the money cerebral cortex, provided by Mark Pinsk, Princeton University. Vertical line shows the plane of the slice shown at bottom. **Bottom:** Drawing of a slice through the brain showing the structures hidden beneath the cortex.

always lying out in the open, waiting for someone to notice them—someone who isn't blinded by prior expectation. Science succeeds only if you are adaptable to the data.

We never did find good results in the claustrum. The neurons didn't behave themselves. They didn't respond crisply to sensory stimuli. Or if they did, we didn't have the right stimuli for them. To this day, the claustrum remains a scientific mystery. But we couldn't help noticing some interesting neurons in a nearby, large brain area that our electrode often skimmed through as we tried to reach the smaller target of the claustrum. The putamen (shown in Figure 5.1) was such a chunky structure, so easy to hit, that we got more data from it than from the claustrum. Science often works that way. You aim for A and discover B.

The putamen is usually considered part of the movement control system. It's one of the most intensely studied structures in the brain because of its involvement in Parkinson's disease, a far-too-common disease that robs people of their ability to move.[3-7] Thousands of scientists around the world are trying to figure out every possible detail of how the putamen works.

If you inject a tiny current through an electrode into one spot in the putamen, buzzing the neurons within a fraction of a millimeter around the electrode tip, you will evoke a muscle twitch on a part of the body.[8] As you lower the electrode in gentle increments, at the top of the putamen you'll find neurons related to the feet.[9] A few millimeters down, further into the putamen, you'll find neurons related to the legs. Then you'll encounter the hips, the torso, the arms, the head, and finally, when the electrode has reached the deepest part of the putamen, you'll find neurons related to the inside of the mouth. The map is neatly laid out, upside down. It's a *homunculus*—a little map of the body in the brain. Or, rather, since we were studying the monkey brain, technically it's called a *simculus*.

Pretty much everyone who studies the putamen studies movement control. But in our experiments, coming from our ill-starred attempt in the claustrum, we were primed to find sensory responses, especially visual responses. We'd listen in on the activity of a neuron and try everything we could think of to make the cell respond. Testing neurons was an exercise in on-the-spot creativity. The enemy was any established assumption that might wall us in and prevent a discovery. This type of experiment is sometimes called a fishing expedition. It's usually frowned on, but every discovery I ever made came out of a fishing expedition. I'm a fan of them.

In the process of fishing, we projected spots and lines and complex pictures on the screen in front of the monkey. We touched his fur with a Q-tip and gently rotated the joints. We played sounds—sine waves, white noise, any random pattern-rich stimulus such as jingling keys or our own voices. I wonder what other people thought, presuming anyone was there at two in the morning passing by the outer door of the lab, hearing us humans imitating monkey whoops. Maybe we sounded like we were getting frisky with each other in the middle of the night.

Gradually, we noticed something peculiar.

As expected, many neurons in the putamen responded as our Q-tip touched the fur. The neurons received information from the touch sensors on the body. But sometimes the neurons began to respond as the Q-tip *approached* the face or arms, before it had touched the fur. That was spooky. Never mind the Q-tip. If you just moved your hand toward the monkey, the neurons would respond. Maybe we were stirring the fur with static electricity or air? No, a clear plastic shield in front of the monkey didn't eliminate the response. But covering the monkey's eyes did. The neurons were evidently visually sensitive. Nobody had ever found visual responses in that part of the brain before.

Two-dimensional visual patterns projected onto a screen had been the mainstay of neuroscience for fifty years and had become an entrenched tradition. When a tradition develops in science, people become blind to its faults. They develop a bias and see the method as correct and proper, simple and controlled. But the images on the screen did a lousy job of activating our putamen neurons. We were going to have to toss out the standard approach and try something different. The neurons responded beautifully to real, three-dimensional objects moving in the space near the body. Any object on a stick worked. A hand is basically an object on a stick, so we used our hands a lot. We also used a toilet brush. We had a drawer full of them. Eventually, we settled on a ping-pong ball duct-taped to the end of a long, thin metal rod.

For people outside of science, this step from a projected image on a screen to a ping-pong ball on a stick may seem trivial. But changes to the tradition can make people's heads explode. Suppose you attended a formal dinner wearing an old pair of sweatpants tied around your neck instead of a tie. To anyone encountering the culture for the first time, the difference would seem trivial enough. It's a long, thin cloth that keeps your neck warm, right? But inside the culture, the innovation would cause confusion, derision, offense—that dude's gone off the rails. This was the spirit of the reaction from many of our scientific colleagues at the time. Not only did we show up to the party with a ping-pong ball on a stick instead of a spot of light on a screen, but we were finding visual responses in a part of the brain where they weren't supposed to exist.

I have a special fondness for the phrase "off the rails." I like it because it shows how easily people forget the actual purpose of science. The purpose is to gain new insight. Rails are engineered to go from point A to point B along a known path. If you're on the rails, in the railway car, you can be sure of one thing: you're not discovering anything. It isn't science. There is no such thing as on-the-rails science. The only way to gain new insight is to go off the rails.

I admit, it's messy. You go through ditches and brambles and mud. The people on the train look out the window at you and shake their heads. I don't know what they're doing in there. Hobnobbing? Playing a game of popularity? I imagine them talking in posh British accents and sipping expensive wines, giving each other merit awards. Meanwhile, I'm having all the fun, bushwhacking and exploring a new direction.

Over months of experimentation in that dark room drenched in leaked anesthesia and listening to a constant clicking of neurons, we pieced together a pattern.[10] Most neurons in the putamen, about seventy-five percent, had what is called a *tactile receptive field*. The definition of a tactile receptive field is the region on the body that, when touched, causes the neuron to respond. Each neuron had its own receptive field, its own little territory that it monitored on the surface of the body. For some neurons, the receptive field was small. It might cover the palm, or a part of the right cheek, or a dollar-bill-sized patch on the torso. Other neurons had larger receptive fields covering an entire arm, half the head, or even half the body. In most cases, the receptive field was located on the side of the body opposite the neuron. Each side of the brain represented the opposite side of the body. But, on occasion, we found receptive fields that were so large they crossed the midline. A few neurons had receptive fields that encompassed every part of the monkey, both sides included.

A smaller proportion of neurons, about thirty-five percent, also responded to the sight of objects near the body. They were sensitive through touch *and* vision. Some examples are shown in Figure 5.2.

These multisensory neurons had three key properties.

First, the tactile responses were astonishingly sensitive. Touch one hair, barely bend it, and you'd trigger a fierce volley of activity in the neuron. In retrospect, maybe we should have known that these neurons constituted a warning system. They were shouting, "Yow! Something just touched me there!"

Second, only neurons with a tactile receptive field that included the face, the arms, or the upper torso had a visual response. Neurons with a tactile receptive field confined to the legs or the tail never had a visual response, at least that we could find. It is possible that the sphinx posture of the monkey on the table contributed to that finding. Visual information was attached to the parts of the body that were close to or in the animal's field of view.

Third, the visual response closely matched the location of the tactile response. If the neuron responded to touching the left cheek, it would respond to the sight of an object in the space near the left

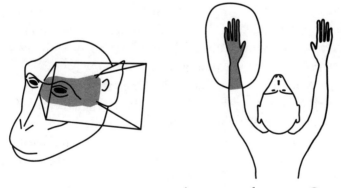

FIGURE 5.2 Typical sensory responses of peripersonal neurons. One neuron responded to a touch on the left side of the face around the eye (shaded area shows the region responsive to touch) and to the sight of objects near the left side of the face (boxed area shows the visually responsive region). Another neuron responded to a touch on the left arm and hand and to the sight of objects in the space near the hand.

cheek. If it responded to touching the top of the head, it would respond to the sight of objects in the upper space near the forehead. The response was especially strong to objects moving toward the body on a collision course with the tactile receptive field. If we positioned the ping-pong ball far away from the body and then brought it slowly closer, the neuron would fire off signals at a faster and faster rate as the ball approached, and then fire in a final frenzy of activity as the ball touched the fur. If we covered the animal's eyes as a sanity check, of course, we'd get no response at all as the ball approached, and the same frenzy of activity as the ball made contact with the fur.

By systematically moving the ping-pong ball around the animal we could plot a visually responsive region for each neuron. That responsive region, or visual receptive field, was a volume like an inflated balloon glued to the body surface, jutting into personal space. For some neurons, the balloon was small. The neuron responded only if an object moved within a few centimeters of the skin. For other neurons, the balloon was much larger, extending outward half a meter or more.

The neurons were monitoring bubbles of space around the body.

One night, about a year into that first series of experiments on the putamen, we made a seemingly trivial observation. It was so obvious, we almost breezed right by it without paying attention. But it nagged at our minds over the next couple days. As we thought about it, we realized that it was not so obvious after all. It might even be the most astonishing feature that we had found yet.

The observation went like this. One neuron that we studied responded to touching the right hand. Its tactile receptive field was shaped like a glove, rather neatly covering the hand and wrist. It also had a good response to the sight of objects in the space near the hand, within about ten centimeters. Since the monkey was deeply anesthetized, lying on the table in a sphinx posture, the hand was resting on the tabletop in the animal's lower right field of view. That was where the visual response was obtained. Any object looming near that part of space revved up the neuron. Out of curiosity, we readjusted the arm and placed the monkey's hand in a central location, jutting into his view near the snout. Now that the hand was in a different part of the animal's field of view, what would happen to the sensory responses? The neuron still responded to a touch on the hand and to the sight of objects looming near the hand. The visual response had followed the hand, moving to the central space. Yet the eyes hadn't moved. The monkey was anesthetized and the eye position was fixed.

We had to think about that for a moment. The visually responsive bubble of space had moved with the hand, as though it were a balloon glued to the skin.

We then tucked the hand out of the monkey's sight, along the side of the body. In that configuration, the neuron still responded to a touch on the hand, but the visual response disappeared altogether. No matter how objects loomed in front of the monkey, the neuron was silent.

These neurons, it seemed, were not just looming detectors, triggering a general alarm when anything came close to the body. They were tracking the location of specific body parts and monitoring the proximity of intruding objects with respect to those body parts. That kind of tracking and monitoring must have required some pretty impressive computational machinery.

We found only five neurons with an arm-tracking style of response in the putamen.[10] We presumably would have found more if we had been searching all along, but it didn't occur to us to test for that property until late in the experiment. It was our first hint of the sophistication of these near-space neurons, and it launched two decades of experiments.

When you encounter a puzzler in your own experiments, you experience a unique moment of relief when you comb through the literature and find out that you're not alone. The findings start to make sense in a larger context.

Neurons that monitor the space around the body through touch and vision can be found in at least three other brain areas in addition to the putamen. These brain areas, shown in Figure 5.3, are directly connected to each other in an information-sharing network.[11-14] That near-space network, first discovered and detailed in the monkey brain, was eventually confirmed in the human brain, as I'll describe in Chapter 9. We all contain something like this mechanism: a patchy neural network linked across the cortical surface and the deep parts of the brain, processing the space on and near the body.

(a)

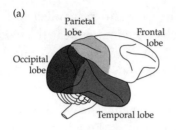

(b)

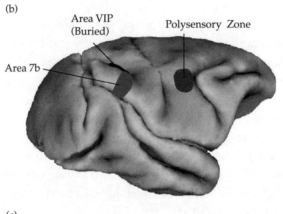

(c)

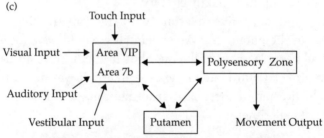

FIGURE 5.3 The peripersonal network in the monkey brain. **A:** Lobes of the cerebral cortex. **B:** Some areas in the cortex with peripersonal neurons. VIP stands for ventral intraparietal and is buried in a fold of the cortex. Image of monkey cortex provided by Mark Pinsk, Princeton University. **C:** Diagram of some of the connections of the peripersonal network.

Area 7b

In the 1970s, Juhani Hyvarinen and his colleagues working in Helsinki made a strange discovery.[15–18] They were studying neurons in a region of the cerebral cortex of monkeys called *area 7b*. Figure 5.3 shows the location of 7b in the parietal lobe. The neurons in 7b responded to a light touch on the fur. Each neuron had a tactile receptive field on the body, usually on the face or arms.

Maybe the experimenters had bright lights trained on the monkey to see what they were doing. At any rate, they noticed that some of the neurons responded when a shadow passed across the tactile receptive field. That must have been a spooky moment. Other neurons responded when any object loomed near the tactile receptive field. The neurons evidently responded through both touch and vision.[15-18]

Area VIP

In the early 1990s, Michael Goldberg and his colleagues working at the National Institutes of Health (NIH) discovered similar neurons in another subregion of the parietal lobe.[19] This area is called the *ventral intraparietal area (VIP)* and is also shown in Figure 5.3. Hyvarinen's area 7b and Goldberg's area VIP are probably continuous, belonging to a single larger cluster of neurons that monitor the space on and immediately around the body. Area VIP has been extensively studied since the 1990s.[20-31] These VIP neurons not only combine touch with vision, but they also respond to sounds near the body.[32] They provide a complete multisensory radar of nearby space.

One of the most intriguing findings from VIP is that the neurons are sensitive to the internal, vestibular sense of head motion.[33-36] If the monkey is put on a platform that can tilt and turn in the dark, the neurons in VIP are affected in complex ways, their responses ramping up or down. Exactly how the vestibular input interacts with the visual, tactile, and auditory input is not yet understood. However, it seems likely that aligning vision, sound, and touch requires some sense of where your head is angled. The vestibular inputs may have something to do with building and maintaining the multisensory map of space.

The Polysensory Zone in the Motor Cortex

The credit for discovering near-space neurons really should go to Giacomo Rizzolatti and his colleagues, since they gave the most complete early description.[37-42] In the 1980s, working in Parma, they discovered what they called "peripersonal" neurons in a region of the motor cortex, which lies in the frontal lobe and is part of the movement control machinery of the brain. Rizzolatti's term for the neurons caught on, and now almost everyone who studies the space near the body refers to peripersonal space and peripersonal neurons.

It has been said that neuroscientists would rather share toothbrushes than share brain area names. The brain region that Rizzolatti studied has at least three names: F4, inferior area 6, and the ventral premotor cortex. These names refer to different proposed ways to subdivide the motor cortex. However, the region where the peripersonal neurons are most common does not perfectly correspond to any of those subdivisions. I eventually coined the term "polysensory zone"[43] to refer in a neutral way to the region of the motor cortex in which the peripersonal neurons are numerous. Whether the polysensory zone belongs within F4, area 6, the ventral premotor cortex, or all of the above is not of great interest to me. Instead, the properties of neurons in the polysensory zone are sensationally interesting to me, and I've spent years studying them.

In the early 1990s, I felt like I was standing in front of a scrumptious buffet. It was full of enticing peripersonal dishes here and there around the brain and I had to decide which dish to dip into first. The putamen was always a little hard to study because it was buried deep in the brain. It's easier to study surface areas, so my collaborators and I focused our research on that enticing little spot, the polysensory zone near the front of the brain—although we put some tracks into areas VIP and 7b, too.

We decided to switch from anesthetized to awake monkeys. We clearly had hold of a dynamic process related to the control of movement, and studying it in a sleeping animal on a tabletop seemed counterproductive.

Studying neurons in an awake monkey is technically challenging, but not impossible. It has long since become routine in neuroscience. The most basic methods were worked out for medical purposes in humans. If you need that type of intervention, first a surgery is performed to outfit you with a port that allows electrodes to be introduced easily into your brain. After you wake up from surgery, doctors can monitor your brain activity for weeks, probing your brain with electrodes, testing for abnormal events such as epileptic seizures. Since there are no pain or touch receptors in the brain, you can't even feel the electrodes in there.

By applying the same general technique to a monkey, researchers can measure the activity of neurons while the monkey sits upright and awake in a specialized monkey chair, pressing buttons, solving tasks, or observing sensory events. For us and our monkeys, the method was a boon and a significant improvement in quality of life. Without the anesthetic leaking into the room we were all more alert, our brains a lot healthier. The monkey was trained to look at a dim spot of light for a few seconds at a time to stabilize his eyes, for which he was paid in squirts of apple juice delivered through a metal straw. Every day, the monkey would come out of the home colony, sit in the experimental apparatus, do his job for a few hours, get paid, and then go back home.

During these daily sessions, when we isolated the electrical signal from a neuron, we'd put that cell through a battery of tests for an hour or two. The tests required a good rapport with the monkey. We'd have to cover his eyes with a black felt blindfold—the "reverse Batman" we called it, because it made him look like a superhero with a confused costume designer. While he was blindfolded, we'd touch him gently all over his furry body to find the neuron's tactile receptive field, and at the same time keep him happy by feeding him raisins. Then we'd uncover his eyes and test the neuron's visual responses with our ping-pong ball duct-taped to the end of a long stick. We added a robot to the mix, a massive mechanical arm hidden behind a black drape that moved the ping-pong ball along specific, controlled trajectories. We named the robot René Descartes.

The monkey and René had a troubled relationship. Sometimes when the robot was doing its job, the monkey would snatch the ball off the end of the stick and stuff it in his mouth, all in one fast gesture, then glare at us as though daring anyone to take his new chew toy away. We had a drawer full of spare ping-pong balls.

With this unlikely collection—René the robot, ping-pong balls, a black felt blindfold, monkeys, and a small group of humans eagerly crowding around the equipment with a notebook and a pencil—we set out to study the network of peripersonal neurons in the brain.

* * *

Scientists are always under pressure to publish papers at a high rate. Each paper is a chance to show off our technical chops. Actual scientific insight isn't always prioritized or incentivized and is sometimes accidentally lost along the way. That's my curmudgeonly impression, anyway.

Most of neuroscience follows a standard operating procedure. First, based on your reading of the literature and your own past results, you propose a general hypothesis, perhaps something like: brain area X performs function Y. Then you design a specific experiment to test that hypothesis. Often a group of people argue and tweak the experimental plan for months, adding complexity. Nobody wants to launch an experiment until every contingency has been considered, every detail anticipated. The goal of the experiment is to turn the initial hypothesis into a specific, numerical prediction. For example: these particular neurons will be twice as active in condition A than in condition B, but only in the presence of C. Once everyone agrees on the plan, you build the equipment, which can take months; train the animal to perform an elaborate task, which can take upwards of a year; collect the data, which can take a few years; and analyze it according to plan. Given the infinite universe of possibilities and the incredibly low likelihood that your original hypothesis lines up with reality, many experiments yield ambiguous results. Maybe the neurons are just as active in condition A as in condition B, and are significantly less active in the presence of C. What does that mean? It doesn't line up with your previous hypothesis *or* your clever counter-hypotheses. You're left trying to extract a useful lesson, which is an art form unto itself. The process is fraught with anxiety. Most scientists would never dream of wasting effort on an open-ended fishing expedition because it isn't directed toward a specific, publishable result.

My own experiments on the peripersonal neurons followed an extravagantly different playbook, an older style that was much more popular before about 1980 but that mainly died out with the rising pressures of the modern scientific marketplace. I followed a two-stage cycle. First, go fishing. Second, take out the calipers and measure the fish.

In the first stage, we'd spend a few months exploring the neurons without making any formal measurements. Nothing was publishable; nothing was meant to be. Every day we'd keep our eyes open. We'd try dozens of mini-tests, anything we could think of on the spot, filling notebooks with hundreds of pages of observations and sketches. We'd pull out amazing fishes of bizarre shapes and colors that nobody had ever imagined before—like the spatial bubbles glued to the hand.

After a while, we'd develop a sense of what kind of fish lived in that part of the brain. When we stopped surprising ourselves every day, when we thought we knew what was going on, we'd shift to the second stage: measuring the fish in a formal, controlled manner. By that time, we understood exactly how to design our experiments. We knew what questions to ask and how to ask them. What is the point of building complicated equipment and designing a beautifully controlled study, only to find out that your hypotheses are orthogonal to reality and the results are uninterpretable—neither entirely right nor wrong? With our two-stage approach, we could gently feel our way close to the underlying reality first, and then design the experiments, build the equipment, and collect the data with confidence.

After a few months of formal experiments and paper writing, we'd publish the results. Other scientists were often as astounded reading our papers as we were when we first encountered the properties of neurons in the lab. I can't count how many times someone asked me, "How did you know to test for that property? How did you even *think* of it?" The answer was, I didn't have to. We went fishing for ideas with a notebook and a brain area full of neurons. We caught the fish first, made our formal measurements second. Then we'd start the cycle again. We'd go fishing and collect a new set of qualitative observations worth testing.

I've never found a better method of scientific discovery. If it hadn't been for that two-stage approach, I'd still be trying to get those neurons to respond to spots of light on a computer screen. I would understand nothing about them. I would have elaborate theories, impressively complex experimental designs, well-trained monkeys pressing buttons and pulling levers, probably a whole stack of papers with enough technical showmanship to get into the most respected journals. But insight? Probably not so much.

For ten years, through the 1990s, my colleagues and I studied that network of multisensory neurons. "Bubble-wrap neurons," I sometimes called them—neurons that monitor bubbles of space wrapped around the body. I like to think those experiments helped to change the way scientists understand the brain.

Chapter 6

Kissing in the Dark

T O A NEUROSCIENTIST, A BRAIN AREA IS LIKE A COUNTRY. It's vast. It fosters a rich intellectual culture. Hundreds, maybe thousands of nerds around the world are busy studying the same brain area, debating its details at conferences. Then you meet someone from outside neuroscience all together. They ask you what you work on and you find yourself describing a spot on a monkey's brain no larger than a tick. That's your life. It's a humbling jolt in perspective. I spent ten years studying the polysensory zone in the motor cortex of the monkey brain.

Why study the monkey brain at all? Monkeys make a good experimental model for the human brain. They don't have very human-like cognition, so perhaps you need more than a grain of salt to study monkey higher-order thought. But they have a very human-like visual system, somatosensory system, and movement control system. The details may be different in a monkey, but the broad outlines turn out to be similar. Almost everything known about these systems in the human was first discovered in the monkey.

The monkey motor cortex is traditionally carved into many subdivisions labeled with cryptic acronyms. Figure 6.1 shows only a few of those subdivisions. Something like fifty have been designated at one time or another. The subdivisions are convenient for scientists, but nobody should ever mistake a lot of boundaries and acronyms

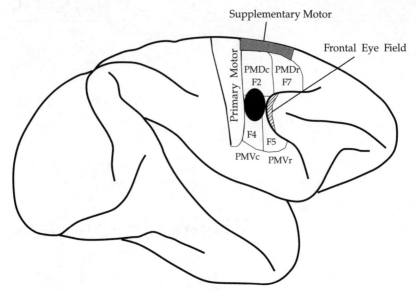

FIGURE 6.1 Some movement control areas of the monkey cerebral cortex. The black oval indicates the approximate location of the polysensory zone in which visual and tactile peripersonal neurons were concentrated. PM = premotor cortex; PMDc = premotor, dorsal, caudal, also sometimes called field 2 or F2; PMDr = premotor, dorsal, rostral, also sometimes called F7; PMVc = premotor, ventral, caudal, also sometimes called F4; PMVr = premotor, ventral, rostral, also sometimes called F5.

for actual deep understanding. The motor cortex remains mysterious. It's probably not really made up of separate areas adjacent to each other with clean borders between them.

Roughly in the center of the motor cortex lies a cluster of neurons that have dual, tactile, and visual responses. As I noted in Chapter 5, these sensory neurons were first discovered in the early 1980s by Rizzolatti and his colleagues.[1-3] I studied them in the 1990s as a researcher in Dr. Gross's lab.[4-12] The neurons were controversial from the start, because what are sensory responses doing in the motor cortex? In traditional neuroscience, sensory responses are in the back half of the brain and movement control is in the front half.

To get a better handle on the multisensory neurons, we did a survey of that cortical region in a group of monkeys.[11] Figure 6.2 shows the result for one monkey who was typical of the group. The cluster of tactile and visual neurons sprawled right in the middle of the

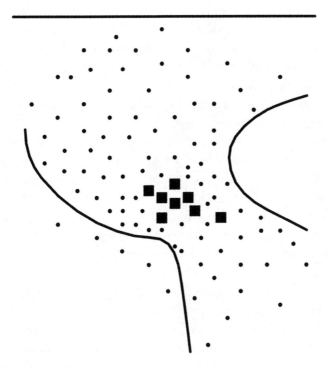

FIGURE 6.2 The polysensory zone as measured in one monkey. Its exact location can vary slightly from one individual to the next. The motor cortex is located between two cortical folds (see Figure 6.1). Every point indicates a tested site in the cortex. Black squares indicate sites where the polysensory, visual, and tactile responses of peripersonal neurons were found. (Adapted from Graziano and Gandhi [2000].[11])

traditional motor cortex map. We called it the "polysensory zone." It isn't really a discrete area because it frays out at the edges. It looks like bees clustered around a hive. It's as if the similar functional properties of these neurons drew them magnetically together during the self-organizing development of the cortex. In cartoon form it's convenient to draw a circle on the brain and say, there, that's the municipality. But the underlying reality is more complicated.

I'll describe one particular neuron as an example. We isolated its signal with the electrode and then began to test its properties. First we put on the monkey's reverse Batman—the felt strip that covered the eyes. At the same time, we gave him a few raisins. He had long since learned to be patient with the procedure. Then we stroked his fur until we found the location of the tactile receptive field on the body. This neuron responded on the left side of the snout. It had a massive response. The clicking of the neuron rose from a baseline of perhaps one or two spikes per second to about a hundred per second. It sounded like an explosion over our loudspeaker.

The neuron was sensitive to direction. If we gently touched a Q-tip to the fur, we evoked a brief response. If we stroked the Q-tip from the center of the face toward the ear, the neuron went crazy, responding at its highest level. If we reversed and stroked the Q-tip back toward the center of the face, abruptly the response stopped and the neuron went silent. If we stroked up toward the eye or down toward the mouth, we evoked a weak response, perhaps about twenty clicks per second.

Then we took the felt covering from the monkey's eyes, and gave him another few raisins in appreciation for his patience. With the eyes open, the neuron responded robustly as the Q-tip approached the left cheek. This particular neuron responded only when we had invaded the space within about ten centimeters. It was an ultra-near neuron. The visual response was direction sensitive, just like the tactile response. If we held the Q-tip near the face and gently moved it from the midline toward the ear, passing through the visually responsive region of space, the neuron crackled. The response was not quite as intense as the tactile response—perhaps about fifty clicks per second. If we stopped and reversed direction, moving the Q-tip back toward the midline of the face, the response stopped dead.

The neuron was not just a proximity detector; it was monitoring the specific *trajectory* of nearby objects. With a million neurons like this, each one sensitive to a different region of space and a different direction of motion, the polysensory zone could keep elaborate track of objects on, near, and distant from the body, with a relative emphasis on the space within about arm's length. Will the object touch me? What part of my body will it hit? Will it pass by to my right or left? Is it moving fast or slow? This is the kind of information processed in the polysensory zone. It's almost like air traffic control for personal space.

At first glance the neurons might seem like a lousy system for locating nearby objects. Their receptive fields are so large that they don't give much spatial specificity. If a neuron revs up, an object must be somewhere within the corresponding large bubble of space. That's the best a single neuron can indicate. But a population of these multisensory neurons with overlapping receptive fields can give much more refined spatial information. This trick of using a pattern of activity among many neurons is sometimes called a "population code."

Figure 6.3 shows a cartoon of many different visual receptive fields corresponding to a diverse sample of neurons. Some of the receptive fields are small, hugging the skin. Others are large, extending out even beyond reaching distance. The combination of these many receptive fields, overlapping like a Venn diagram, would, in principle, be able to monitor the exact location of objects around the body.

The near space, within reaching distance, is heavily represented by about 95 percent of the neurons. More distant space, out to many meters if not farther (the size of our room limited the experiment), is thinly represented by only about five percent of the neurons. In

FIGURE 6.3 Schematic illustration of the overlapping visually responsive regions for many peripersonal neurons. Although the peripersonal mechanism emphasizes the space near the body, some neurons also monitor more distant space.

general, cells that monitored a small tactile zone on a specific part of the body also monitored a small visual zone restricted to the space near the body. Cells that monitored a large tactile zone that covered most or all of the body tended to have a large visual zone that extended out as far as we could test. Many authors have incorrectly described the peripersonal mechanism in the brain as strictly limited to reaching distance, a simplification that may have biased people's intuitions about the functional use of these neurons. In reality, the mechanism greatly *emphasizes* the space near the body but processes distant space as well.

In retrospect, I wish I had studied smell. One of the most vivid ways we judge intrusions into personal space is by smell (especially body odor). I'm reminded of a fabulous and underappreciated novel, *The Sunlight Dialogues,* by John Gardner.[13] The Sunlight Man was a magician with an uncanny habit of appearing near you without warning. You knew he was in the room only because his terrible smell would suddenly overwhelm you. You'd turn around and see him lounging in a nearby chair. But odorants are difficult to control, especially if the key variable in the experiment is spatial location, so perhaps it's just as well that we didn't try to waft odors at the monkey.

I also wish I had studied the sense of balance—the vestibular signals from the inner ear that track head movements. Frank Bremmer and his colleagues discovered vestibular signals among the peripersonal neurons of cortical area VIP.[14–16] These signals may be important for aligning the visual space near the head with the tactile space on the head. In my guess, they play a crucial role in how the peripersonal neurons construct their response properties in the first place. However, those discoveries came a decade later, in the early 2000s. At the time we began to study the polysensory zone, in the 1990s, it didn't occur to us to tilt or rotate the monkey's chair. To date, nobody has studied vestibular signals in the polysensory zone.

But we did study another sense, outside of vision and touch, that's also crucial for personal space: hearing. About five years into our experiments I noticed what seemed to be crinkly glove neurons. If I stood behind the monkey and reached into the space just behind his head, gently rubbing my fingers together, the exam glove would make a faint crinkling sound. Some of the neurons responded to that sound.

We were already in trouble with the traditionalists over visual responses in a motor area and especially over non-standard stimuli such as Q-tips and ping-pong balls. I remember a distinct wilting feeling when I first noticed the crinklyglove response. I was adjusting a piece of equipment behind the monkey's head when the neuron began to fire. I tried it two or three times, found a consistent pattern, and thought something like, "Oh frick! Another weird complexity that nobody's going to believe."

In the end, the auditory neurons made wonderful sense.[9] They were not that complicated. They made me think of a mosquito whining past my ear. The brain evidently had a mechanism for monitoring nearby objects by sound. The responses were mostly associated with the space near the back of the head, a zone that vision obviously cannot monitor.

To give one example, we found a neuron in the polysensory zone that had a tactile response on the left side of the head. The receptive field included a bit of the left cheek, the left ear, and the back left part of the head. Since part of the tactile receptive field wrapped onto the front of the face, we expected the neuron to have a visual response, and it did. The neuron responded to the sight of objects in the space near the left side of the face.

But the tactile receptive field also wrapped around onto the back of the head. Clearly, vision couldn't monitor the space near the back of his head. Perhaps because of that, the same neuron responded to sound. We could get a small response from a sound coming from anywhere—near, far, right, left—but only sounds generated in the space directly behind the left side of the head evoked a strong response. Any type of sound would do—a voice, a clap, a sine wave— but hissing static and high-pitched clicks worked best.

If the sound was far away, no matter how loud it was, it evoked little response. Even the faintest whisper, if it was nearby, would drive a robust response. To convince ourselves of this distance sensitivity, we had to put a small microphone in the monkey's ear to measure the sound. We ringed the monkey with speakers at various distances and angles and presented sounds at a great range of amplitudes, from inaudible to stentorian. Sure enough, once all the numbers had been crunched, the neuron responded best to sounds within about twenty centimeters of the left back part of the head, regardless of how loud or soft.

Like so many other properties of the multisensory neurons, this preference for nearby sounds seemed so natural that we almost shrugged it off as obvious and moved on. Then, in one of those head-scratching moments, we thought about it more deeply. How does a neuron know the distance to the sound source, if not by the amplitude of the sound? How can the system tell that the quiet, crinkly glove sound came from just behind the head? How does it know to respond to the quiet hiss of white noise from a speaker a hand's-breadth behind the head, and yet ignore the same white noise when it is located an arm's length from the back of the head and the loudness is adjusted so that the amplitude at the ear is the same?

Auditory space is probably the most difficult, computationally intensive space for the brain to construct. Tactile space is easy in comparison. If there's a touch on the hand, then something is on your hand. There's a one-to-one correspondence between the location of the sensory neuron and the location of the relevant object in the world. But if there's a sound nearby, the sound waves spread everywhere and enter both ears. Auditory space requires a lot of hard preprocessing of the data. Of course, it doesn't seem like that to our conscious minds. Perceptually, the sound seems to come from *there*. Behind that perception is a lot of hidden computation.

Some aspects of auditory space are reasonably well understood.[17] To calculate whether the sound comes more from the left or the right, the brain must compare the two ears. Is the sound louder in the right ear or the left? Did it reach the right ear a few microseconds before it reached the left? Precise circuits in the brainstem perform those delicate computations.

Much less is known about how the brain reconstructs the *distance* to a sound.[17] A range of studies suggests that we rely on reverberation. Subtle echoes tell us about the size of the space around us and the distance to a sound source. We all intuitively know the sonic difference between an echoing cathedral and a closet full of old clothes. The space is alive in one case and totally dead in the other. Even with your eyes closed you can sense that largeness or smallness. The same subtle reverberation cues are used to parse out the distance to a voice or a footstep.

One of the hints that reverberation lies at the root of distance perception comes from animals that are true experts at three-dimensional auditory perception: bats and dolphins. They evolved echolocation, which is really just a souped-up version of reverberation analysis. They generate a sound pulse and analyze the returning echo.

People also have a version of echolocation, though we are novices compared to bats.[18-20] It used to be called "facial vision" before anybody knew what it was.[18] If you blindfold someone and tell her to walk carefully forward and stop before hitting an obstacle, she'll probably manage to stop before disjointing her nose on a wall. She won't necessarily know how she does it. People report feeling something like a warning prickle on the face or a shadow in their minds.

I'm reminded of a short story by Roald Dahl, *The Wonderful Story of Henry Sugar*.[21] It's about a mystic who develops his facial vision to an amazing degree. In a moment of hubris he has wads of dough plopped over his eyes and then linen wrapped around and around his head until he looks like a mummy from the neck up. To the astonishment of the spectators, he gets on a bicycle and weaves effortlessly in and out of traffic. Well, that's fiction. And it's Roald Dahl, too, so we can expect the exaggeration.

In reality, facial sense can give you a vague impression of nearby looming objects. It can also be blocked by a simple intervention. If the mystic had put the dough in his ears he would have been hopeless getting around. Facial sense, when put to experimental test, depends on subtle sounds generated by the body—breathing, rustling of clothes—and the reverberation of those sounds from nearby surfaces.[18-20] We don't consciously realize that it has anything to do with sound. That processing is somehow under the surface of awareness. The experience seems more like a spooky kind of shadow vision without eyes, or like a subtle warmth on the face.

The personal-space neurons that we studied, with their auditory and visual responses extending into the space around the head, joined to a strong tactile response on the face, begin to sound particularly relevant. I suspect that they form the basis of the mysterious facial sense. The neurons can be triggered by a variety of sensory sources and, once triggered, give a rough map of where objects lie around the body.

We discovered the kissing-in-the-dark neurons by accident. One of the best ways to manipulate vision is to turn the room lights on and off. You can't make a ping-pong ball appear and disappear like pixels on a computer screen, but you can sneak it into place when the lights are off, then switch the lights on and reveal it. So we designed a ball-revealing apparatus.[5] It involved a well-oiled hinge, a ball that could be silently swiveled into place near the monkey's face, and an array of super-bright LEDs, lights that turn on and off with a rise-time of microseconds. We thought we were clever, but the neurons turned out to be way more clever.

We found what seemed like a typical visual and tactile neuron. It responded to a touch anywhere on the left cheek and to the sight of objects anywhere in the space within about fifteen centimeters of the left cheek. Both responses were strong, firing up at about one hundred fifty spikes per second when the face was stimulated. The neuron was a robust radar for objects intruding into that specific region of space. It signaled with such good fidelity that when I closed my eyes and listened to the clicking of the neuron, I could tell without any possible doubt exactly when the other experimenters were looming into that part of the monkey's personal space.

Then we tried our clever manipulation. At first, no object was near the face, and the neuron was quiet. We turned the room lights off, and the neuron continued to be quiet. The room was a cinderblock bunker with no windows and every piece of equipment had its power-light disconnected, so we could achieve a dense darkness. Neither monkey nor experimenters could see anything. Silently— we had practiced it ahead of time so we could manage it in the dark— we swiveled the ping-pong ball on its stick until it reached a fixed position. The ball was parked about five centimeters from the left cheek, in the middle of the visually responsive region of the neuron. The neuron still did not respond. That was a relief. It told us that the monkey truly could see nothing and that the ball wasn't stirring the hairs on his face.

Then we turned on the super-bright LEDs. They lit the scene in a stark, greenish glare, revealing all at once the smuggled-in ping-pong ball and the monkey—looking, as always, unimpressed by the antics of his experimenters.

As soon as the lights revealed the presence of the ball near the face, the neuron began to respond. Its firing rate jumped up tenfold in a period of about a tenth of a second. In effect, the cell was shouting, "Whoa! Hey! Something's in my special bubble of space!" So far, so good. The experiment was working.

Then we turned off the lights. The room was plunged into darkness again. We expected the neuron to shut off. After all, the visual stimulus was gone. But instead, the neuron kept on firing at a high rate. It chugged away as if it were busy telling the rest of the brain, "Yo, don't forget that thing near the cheek. It's probably still there." The system was *remembering* where the object was in the dark. At this point, my mind started to blow.

Maybe, somehow, we had made a mistake and the ball was tickling the face. Maybe the equipment had moved slightly? Or maybe, now that the monkey knew it was there, he could detect a faint outline? That was easy to test. In the dark, we silently swiveled the ball away from the face.

The neuron kept on responding. *It* didn't know that the ball was gone. The monkey didn't know. The peripersonal mechanism didn't register any change in the personal space around the face. The neuron was still shouting out its signal.

Finally, we turned the lights back on. The greenish glare revealed the scene again, this time with no ball near the face. The neuron's bubble of space was empty. At that instant, the neuron went quiet. It seemed to tell the brain, "Oh wait, never mind, dude, false alarm, it's gone."

We could go back and forth revving up the neuron and shutting it down. The response didn't track the *sight* of the object. It wasn't strictly a visual response. It seemed to compute a reasonable guess about the *location* of the object based on the most recent available information.

We did one more manipulation just to push the limits of the system. With the lights on, we swiveled the ball into place near the left cheek, revving up the neuron. Then we turned off the lights, plunging the monkey into darkness, and silently swiveled the object away from the face. Just as before, the neuron continued to fire. The system was maintaining in memory the presence of an object near the cheek. Then we swiveled the monkey's head.

The monkey was sitting in a standard apparatus for testing neurons. A part of the apparatus held his head still. We could adjust the angles, rotating his head gently. In the dark, it must have seemed to the monkey that his head was rotating away from that ball near the left cheek. And sure enough, the neuron fell silent. Either a vestibular signal tracking the movement of the head, or a signal from the neck indicating the angle of the head, fed into that neuron. When we rotated the head back, as though his cheek were moving back toward the ball again, the cell fired up. We could move his head here and there, and as long as his left cheek moved near the remembered location of the ball, the neuron revved up. Finally, we turned the lights on and the monkey saw the trick we had played. The ball had been taken away in the dark a long time ago. Nothing was there. At that point, the neuron went silent, and rotating the head in the light or the dark had no more impact.

The neuron was responding to a complicated construct. If pertinent information suggested that an object was near the left cheek—whether the monkey saw it there, or felt it there, or remembered it in the dark, and whether the object moved toward the monkey or the monkey's head moved toward the object, it was all the same. The neuron signaled the location of that object relative to the face. The system could keep track of objects in the dark. It had what is sometimes called "object permanence."

I thought about all the times I had groped in the dark from my bed to the bathroom while remembering the layout of furniture. Or closed my eyes for a moment at my desk and still knew intuitively not to put my elbow through my Diet Coke. The potential versatility of this brain system was amazing.

After this publication, in 1998, *Glamour* magazine wrote a piece on how we had discovered the mechanism whereby lovers find each other's lips in the dark.[22] I think that must be my career highlight.

Now I'll risk some real complexity.

Visual information by itself is pretty much useless. An image is projected onto the back of the eyes, but the eyes are constantly moving around, the head is moving, the body is moving. It's like putting a video camera on a bucking bronco and trying to analyze that wheeling, shaking image to figure out where anything is in the world.

How does the brain reconstruct the three-dimensional world? If you know where an image falls on your retina, and you also know where your eyes are pointed in your head, in principle, you can do some geometry with those two pieces of information and reconstruct where an object is located with respect to your head.[23–26] You can construct what's sometimes called "head-centered coordinates." If you add in another piece of information, the angle of your head on your trunk, you can, in principle, reconstruct where objects are in trunk-centered coordinates.[27] Basically, with some vector algebra, you can turn a jumping, wheeling retinal image into a spatial map of where objects are located with respect to your body core.

Richard Andersen has done more than any other scientist to tackle how the brain solves this problem. I know his work quite well, since I worked in his MIT lab for two years in the early 1990s, and his ideas influenced much of my later work.

Long before I ever joined his lab, in the 1980s, Andersen began a series of now classic experiments on the parietal lobes of monkeys. He found that neurons in the parietal lobes were sensitive to all the relevant pieces of information for constructing a useful map of visual space.[23-33] The neurons responded to visual images on the retina. They were also influenced by the position of the eyes in the head. Some neurons were even influenced by the angle of the head on the trunk. Any one neuron had such a complicated response profile that its activity gave little clear information about the visual world. If its activity went up or down, one couldn't tell which factor precisely caused the change. Or, to put it differently, if you closed your eyes and listened to the activity of that one neuron, you would never be able to tell exactly what your colleagues were doing around the monkey.

But a population of these neurons, in aggregate, contained substantial information hidden in their complex pattern of activity. If you fed the outputs of a large set of these neurons into a sophisticated computer algorithm, the computer could, in principle, figure out where objects were in real space in reference to the body.[25] Presumably, something in the brain was doing the same thing, using the information from the parietal lobe to reconstruct visual space.[34-37]

The polysensory zone of the motor cortex is definitely one of the brain areas to draw on that information from the parietal lobe and use it to construct space.[2,4,6,38,39] To explain how we know that, I'll describe one of my experiments in some detail. This experiment came relatively late in our study of the peripersonal neurons, when we already had a pretty good sense of their properties and knew how to design an efficient experiment.

Figure 6.4 shows the responses of a typical neuron.[6] It responded to a touch anywhere on the left side of the monkey's snout. It also

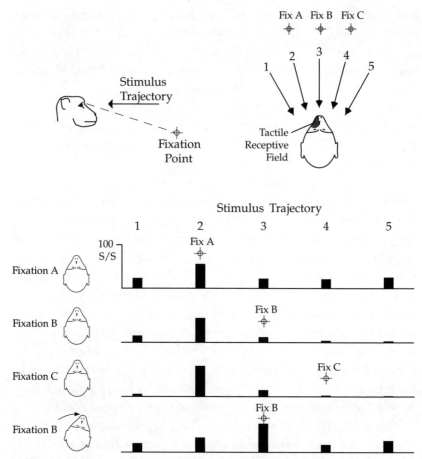

FIGURE 6.4 Activity of a peripersonal neuron with a tactile response on the face and a visual response near the face. The bar graphs show the activity of the neuron in spikes per second (S/S) during the half-second period when the visual stimulus (a ping-pong ball) was moved toward the head. Regardless of where the monkey was looking (Fixation Point A, B, or C), the neuron responded best when the visual stimulus loomed near the tactile receptive field on the left cheek. When the head was facing forward, the visual response was greatest to trajectory 2. When the head was rotated 15 degrees to the right, the visual response was greatest to trajectory 3. Moving the arm had no effect on the visual response. (Adapted from Graziano et al. [1997].[6])

responded to visual stimuli looming near that part of the skin. To test the neuron, we attached our ping-pong ball to René Descartes, the robot, and moved the ball gently along five different trajectories toward the monkey's head. The neuron responded best during trajectory 2, the one that approached the tactile receptive field on the snout.

The monkey was trained to look at a small, dim light for a few seconds at a time. If he did so, he was rewarded with a squirt of apple juice. We had three lights in front of the monkey, and depending on which one we lit up, we could instruct him to look in one direction or another—to the right, to the center, or to the left. The neuron was unaffected by this change in eye position. Whether the monkey looked at light A, B, or C, the neuron always responded best to trajectory 2.

But if we changed the position of the monkey's head, then the response changed. When the head was rotated to the right, the peak of the visual response moved over to trajectory 3.

In one sense, the neuron shown in Figure 6.4 had a very simple response. The neuron cared about a bubble of space extending outward from the left side of the snout, like an invisible balloon glued to the face. Any visual stimulus approaching that part of the face triggered a response, regardless of where the eyes were pointing or the head was angled. In another sense, the response was outrageously complicated. Something was keeping track of the shifting of the eyes and subtracting that motion from the visual information stream.

Figure 6.5 shows an even more complex outcome. Here we tested a neuron that had a tactile response on the right arm. When we touched the fur anywhere on a region of the right arm, the neuron would respond at the onset of the touch. We put the monkey's arm in a padded arm holder so that we could move it into several different positions. Of course, the neuron responded when we first strapped the arm into the arm holder, but the response stopped within a few seconds. This neuron only cared about the onset of touch, perhaps something like the way we soon ignore the feel of our own clothes.[12]

Then we used René Descartes to move the ping-pong ball toward the monkey along four trajectories. In this case, the neuron responded best during trajectory 4, the one that approached closest to the neuron's tactile receptive field on the arm. Whether the monkey looked

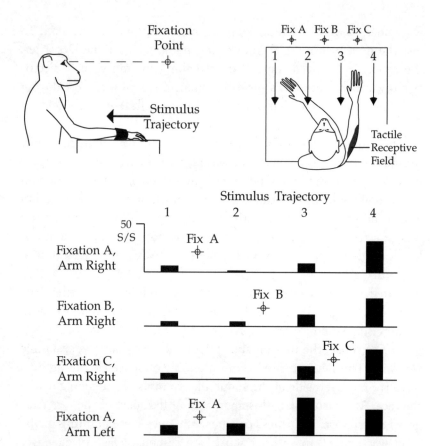

FIGURE 6.5 Activity of a peripersonal neuron with a tactile response on the arm and a visual response near the arm. The bar graphs show the activity of the neuron in spikes per second (S/S) during the half-second period when the visual stimulus (a ping-pong ball) was moved toward the body. Regardless of where the monkey was looking (Fixation Point A, B, or C), the neuron responded best when the visual stimulus loomed near the tactile receptive field on the arm. When the arm was on the right, the visual response was greatest to trajectory 4. When the arm was moved to the left, the visual response was greatest to trajectory 3. Rotating the head had no effect on the visual response. (Adapted from Graziano et al. [1997].[6])

at light A, B, or C made no difference. Whether the monkey's head was angled to the left or right made no difference. But if the arm was moved, then the response changed. When we shifted the arm toward the left, the peak visual response shifted to the left, to trajectory 3. This visual response was anchored to the arm. The neuron was monitoring a bubble of space like an invisible balloon glued to the arm.

These kinds of responses, revealed in the data with the help of our robot, showed the geometric complexity of the neurons. If a neuron had a tactile response on the head, then the volume of visual space that it monitored was head-centered, like a balloon glued to the face. It moved as the head moved. If the neuron had a tactile response on the arm, then the visual space it monitored was arm-centered, like a balloon that was glued to the arm and that moved as the arm moved.

We called it "body-part-centered coordinates."[4] The brain represented the personal space around the body in a manner so complicated, so dynamic, and yet so sensible, it filled us with a special kind of delight that scientists experience when they encounter something elegant in the natural world. Space was like a million balloons of different sizes glued all over the body. Or maybe space was like a Jello mold, deforming and bending as the limbs moved and the head rotated. Body-part-centered coordinates kept track of where objects were with respect to individual body parts. It was a new vision of how the brain constructed personal space.

Now I come to a cautionary tale in scientific hubris.

After more than ten years of experiments, by about the year 2000, I thought I understood these complicated and wonderful neurons. They were sensory neurons in a motor area. They kept track of nearby objects with respect to different parts of the body. Reaching for a hamburger with your hand, reaching toward your lover's lips with your mouth, heading a soccer ball, landing a punch in a boxing match, flinching from a nearby wasp, reaching toward your pen while snaking your arm around a coffee cup—pretty much all visually guided movements of the limbs, trunk, or head could be chalked up to the spatial guidance of these body-part-centered neurons. So I thought, anyway. Maybe I should have suspected that something was amiss when a tick-sized spot in the brain seemed responsible for most of the animal's behavior.

I designed a simple experiment to show how these neurons were involved in locating and then reaching toward nearby objects. At least some encouraging hints in the early literature suggested that they might be involved in this type of sensory-guided reaching.[3] I imagined my experiment would take a few months, give us the obvious, expected results, confirm my safe assumptions, and wrap up a decade-long scientific story.

Here's the experiment. The monkey was trained to press and hold a button (button 1) directly in front of him for about five seconds. If he performed correctly, he was given a squirt of apple juice into his mouth through a metal straw. Monkeys love apple juice, so he was eager to do his part. While his hand was stationary, a second button (button 2) moved toward him from about a meter away to an easy reaching distance. Button 2 was mounted on the end of a stick and controlled by René Descartes the robot. As soon as button 2 stopped moving, the monkey was supposed to release button 1, reach toward button 2, and press it. He would then be rewarded with the apple juice. After a few months of training the monkey became an expert at the task, running hundreds of trials a day, pressing, waiting, reaching, pressing.

The idea was simple. Each neuron should give a burst of activity as the monkey saw button 2 approaching the arm. This response would show that the neuron was monitoring the visual space that the button had just entered. The neuron should give a second burst of activity as the monkey's hand lifted from button 1 and reached toward button 2, showing that the same neuron helped to control the reach. Sensory and motor, see and reach—both responses demonstrated in the same neuron. It was the crucial experiment to show that the peripersonal neurons located objects near the body and guided movements toward those objects.

Right away we realized that something was wrong. The neurons fell silent during the trained task. For example, I found a neuron with a beautiful strong tactile response whenever we touched the forearm and a good visual response to any object looming into the space near the forearm. We started up the task and the neuron simply stopped firing. We programmed our robot so that button 2 moved directly over the forearm, into the heart of the neuron's responsive bubble of space. The neuron should have revved up, but instead, it didn't react. When the monkey lifted his hand from button 1 and moved it to press button 2, we had no luck again. No response.

We wondered if we had lost the neuron, if somehow the electrode had jiggled past it and we were no longer able to pick up the signal, so we stopped the task and tried our simple ping-pong ball on a stick. The response came back. There was the neuron.

We started up the task again, and as soon as the monkey started pressing and reaching, the neuron went silent.

None of our multisensory neurons participated in the reaching task. They seemed to have nothing whatsoever to do with guiding a reach toward a nearby target. They shut down when the monkey was performing the task.

I was stumped. The result contradicted years of assumptions. It also contradicted earlier observations from other researchers, in which peripersonal neurons became active during reaching movements[3] (a mystery we eventually solved, as I'll describe in Chapter 8). I was sure I was probing the brain's mechanism for visually guided behavior. So why didn't it work?

I spun a lot of complicated explanations. Maybe we had overtrained the monkey and the task was now so automatized that the motor cortex had shut down and some other, more primitive part of the brain had taken over. Well, that sounded like a stretch. I had never heard of anything like that before in a reaching task. Neuroscientists had been using reaching tasks for decades, and all the expected brain areas participated. But here we had a clear negative result. The personal space neurons were not involved in reaching.

We never did publish those results. Negative results usually don't interest the journals. More's the pity. If we had been able to publish them, maybe someone else less blinded by assumptions and expectations would have spotted the explanation. As it was, it would be years before we understood the reasons why that experiment had failed.

Then we stumbled upon the "biblical" cells.[12] That's the name we gave them, anyway. They represented another strange phenomenon that contradicted my assumptions.

Here's how the biblical cells worked. Usually we tested the multisensory neurons with simple objects—a ping-pong ball, a Q-tip, nothing complicated. One day—and I honestly can't remember what put the thought into our heads—we were testing the neurons with a realistic plastic apple and a realistic rubber snake, both mounted on sticks. The monkey reacted to the two objects rather differently.

He wanted the apple. He stared at it and cooed, asking for the treat. Monkeys have a way of raising their eyebrows, smacking their lips, and hooting, which is their version of puppy dog eyes. He didn't respond as overtly to the snake, but he kept his eyes on it warily. Monkeys are rumored to be afraid of snakes, even monkeys who are raised in captivity, as though the fear were genetically built into them. I couldn't tell if that was the case here, but the strange rubber object certainly did not entice the monkey.

We found a neuron with a tactile response on the face and a nice strong visual response to any object looming toward the face. Well, as soon as we made that plastic apple loom toward the face, the response went away. The neuron shut off, just like in our reaching task. It was blind to the apple. But if we made the rubber snake loom toward the face, the neuron went crazy. It responded three times more than to a mere ping-pong ball.

It wasn't just one fluke of a neuron. As we tested more neurons with our biblical stimuli, we found the same result. The response to the apple was always greatly reduced, sometimes absent all together. But the response to the snake went through the roof. It beat all other responses. Peripersonal neurons liked snakes, not apples.

I still couldn't grasp the meaning. I was too invested in my own ideas. I was sure these neurons guided *any* kind of movement. Ducking, reaching, nudging, hitting, putting food in the mouth, anything. It made no sense that the neurons would care more about some nearby objects than others. Or, if a neuron showed any preferences, it ought to have responded more to the apple, the object that the monkey most obviously wanted to grab.

Anyway, on what basis could the neurons distinguish a snake from an apple? Were the neurons somehow shape-sensitive? Color-sensitive? Maybe even face-sensitive, responding to the little eyes and mouth on the rubber snake? Suddenly these neurons seemed to tap into the highest levels of object recognition. What kind of crazy visual responses did we have here? I had jumped into a conceptual disaster. The neurons used to tell a coherent story that I had been presenting in my scientific talks around the world for ten years, and now they had become so complex and unaccountable that nothing made sense.

Another, simpler possibility was available, but I had trouble accepting it. The multisensory neurons in the motor cortex might serve mainly as a defensive shield—a second skin. They might be involved in protecting the body rather than in the more targeted actions of reaching and grasping. In that interpretation, showing a snake raised the protective shields, revving up the neurons. Showing the apple lowered the shields because, after all, you need those shields down to allow the fruit close enough to grab it and eat it. If a neuron had a tactile response on the arm and monitored a region of space surrounding the arm, it should participate in arm movements *away* from the nearby object, not toward it—exactly the opposite of the hypothesis I had tried to test with my ill-fated button-pressing experiment.

I resisted the defensive-shield interpretation. It seemed to devalue my neurons. I didn't want to face the possibility that they were responsible for only half of behavior instead of all of it. As dumb as that sounds in retrospect, I think it pretty nearly captures the emotional reaction running just underneath my clever rationalizations. The defensive hypothesis seemed intuitively wrong to me. It was distasteful. And it contradicted years of speculations and assumptions that I had been writing into my published papers.

I want to say that every scientist makes mistakes, which is certainly true. And I want to say that it's *easy* to make scientific mistakes, which is also true. But there's a less forgiving lesson here: never stop listening to the data. The moment you give more weight to your own "intuitions"—a code word for biases that come from every possible source, legit or not—and decide to pit your clever arguments against the data, you will lose the scientific truth.

Sometimes an experiment comes along that points you right, tearing you away from an accumulation of old assumptions. When I began to head my own lab at Princeton University in the early 2000s, and continued my experiments, I tried a new twist on an old method. We began to stimulate the brain with electrical microcurrents. The stimulation would rev up a clump of neurons near the electrode tip, the neurons would trigger behavior, and we could see right away what those neurons were wired up to do. It was a satisfying, direct approach to the mystery neurons we had been studying for so long.

For the previous ten years we might as well have been wearing that black felt blindfold that we sometimes put on the monkey.

We had understood so little. Finally, with the electrical stimulation experiments, we pulled off the blindfold and could see what was right in front of us. The experiments put a new light on the entire motor cortex, not just the peripersonal neurons, and led to something of a revolution in understanding how the brain controls movement. That story is told in the next chapter.

Chapter 7

Hand-to-Mouth and Other Shocking Surprises of the Motor Cortex

O NE MORNING IN THE SUMMER OF 2000, MY FRIEND and colleague Dr. Tirin Moore came running into my office. I remember he was wearing an unbuttoned white lab coat that billowed behind him like the cape of a superhero. "Mike," he said with breathless excitement, "you have to see this."

I followed him down the hall to his experiment room. The walls were lined with racks of electronic equipment filled with blinking lights, switches, and dials. A standard primate chair was fixed in the center of the room, and in the chair, a small, fuzzy monkey was sitting calmly, waiting for treats.

"Look at this," Tirin said. He held up a square of plastic with a red button in the middle and a wire connecting it to the nearest equipment rack. He pressed the button and the monkey's left hand lifted up to a spot about fifteen centimeters in front of the left shoulder, the fingers and thumb shaped as if to grasp an invisible object. Monkeys sometimes do peculiar things. Maybe he was picking at a piece of floating dust. Maybe it was a coincidence. But no. When the monkey's hand dropped back down to his lap, Tirin pressed the button again. Instantly, the hand came up to the exact same spot, shaped in the same manner.

The monkey seemed about as astonished as we were. After about five button presses, he grabbed his left hand with the right one, yanked it down, and sat on it. That was the end of the experiment for the day.

Tirin was experimenting on a part of the brain called the *frontal eye field*, an area that helps control movements of the eyes and head. For about fifty years, experimenters had been using electrodes and micro-currents to artificially stimulate the frontal eye field, causing shifts in gaze direction.[1-7] Tirin was beginning a long, and what turned out to be quite brilliant, series of studies on this brain area.[8-14] But every monkey had a slightly different brain shape, and to find the right location in each monkey required an initial period of trial and error. It was during that initial mapping on one particular monkey that Tirin had gotten his electrode into an unexpected place. Given such a pronounced movement of the arm, we were pretty sure the electrode was positioned too far back by perhaps a few millimeters and had entered the motor cortex instead of the frontal eye field. And yet even in the motor cortex, evoking such a sophisticated movement, a fully coordinated reach, was unheard of.

To understand how astonished we were, you need to understand some of the scientific background. Applying electrical stimulation to the motor cortex was the single most paradigmatic experiment in the whole of neuroscience. The method had been repeated literally thousands of times over the previous one hundred and thirty years. To stumble on something new in that thoroughly vetted corner of the intellectual landscape was beyond bizarre.

Arguably, modern neuroscience began in 1870 with a watershed experiment.[15] Two German scientists, Gustav Fritsch and Eduard Hitzig, discovered that the cerebral cortex, the mysterious wrinkled meat that covers the surface of the brain, controls movement. At least, one part of it does.

Hitzig had worked as a battlefield surgeon in the Prussian army. He noticed a possible relationship between certain areas of the human cerebral cortex and the control of movement. Intrigued, he and his colleague Fritsch decided to study the matter further in the dog brain. They performed their experiments at home, reputedly using Frau Hitzig's dressing table as an operating surface. Exposing the cortex of a dog, they applied a spark of electrical energy from a hand-cranked electrostatic generator. They adjusted the electrical current until it was just intense enough to be felt when they applied the electrode to their own tongues. By stimulating different spots on the surface of the dog's cortex, they hoped to chase down the strange possibility that the cortex influenced movement.

What they found with their crude techniques revolutionized neuroscience.

When they touched their electrode to a specific site on the cortex near the front of the brain, the dog's back leg twitched. When they stimulated a different, nearby site, the front leg twitched. At another site, the neck muscles contracted and the head twitched.

At the time, almost nothing was known about the functions of the cerebral cortex. Scientists had vague theories about complex, subtle functions such as emotion, belief, and intelligence. To poke that lump of meat and get such a specific reaction must have been beyond astonishing. They must have known in that moment that a new door had been opened in science. People could probe the brain like an engineer probes a machine. One could stimulate different locations and measure the result.

From 1870 to 2000, for one hundred thirty years, literally thousands of scientists repeated that experiment in dozens of animal species, including humans.[16] Electrical stimulation became the method of choice to map the muscles across the motor cortex. It was like plucking the individual strings on a marionette. Each spot in the motor cortex was the source of a different string that passed down, through a relay in the spinal cord, to a specific set of muscles. The feet were represented at the top of the brain, the tongue at the bottom, and the rest of the body was arranged systematically along a strip of cortex in between. The map was not perfect; it contained some overlap, some jumble of muscles. But more or less, the body was etched upside down in the motor cortex.

The most famous version of the map is probably Wilder Penfield's. During the 1920s and 1930s he collected data from human patients.[17] For medical purposes, usually to alleviate epilepsy, he opened the skull under local anesthesia. He probed the surface of the cortex with a handheld electrode, gently shocking this and that spot, mapping out sites in the brain for surgical removal. In the course of his mapping, he made thousands of observations. The patients reported spectacular sensations and memories triggered by the focal electrical stimulation. When the stimulation was applied to the motor cortex, the patients produced muscle twitches. Penfield called the motor map a "homunculus," or little man, in the head and drew the iconic picture of a distorted human with giant hands and lips.[18] Almost every psychology and neuroscience textbook includes his picture (see Figure 7.1).

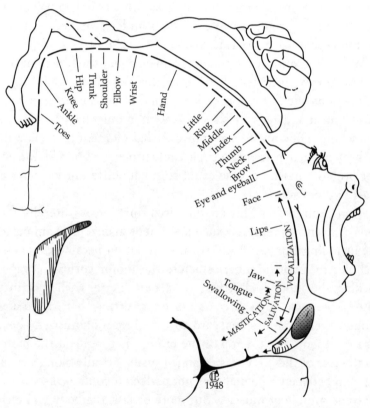

FIGURE 7.1 The motor homunculus in the human brain, from Penfield and Rasmussen.[18] A slice through the motor cortex is shown. Each point in the motor cortex was electrically stimulated and the evoked muscle twitch was noted. Although each cortical point could activate many muscles, a rough body plan could be discerned. (From Penfield and Rasmussen. *The Cerebral Cortex of Man.* © 1950 Gale, a part of Cengage Learning, Inc. Reproduced by permission.)

Now I need to introduce one tiny, crucial detail. Sometimes in science the most absurdly small item can have the biggest impact, upsetting the grandest of theories. In this story of motor cortex, that crucial little detail turned out to be the length of time that the electrical stimulation was applied to the cortex. The traditional method involved extremely brief stimulation—as brief as possible.[16] In the early experiments, such as the dog experiments of Fritsch and Hitzig,[15] the static electricity excited the neurons only in that infinitesimal first moment, the onset of the discharge. In later experiments, when a high-frequency train of electrical pulses was applied to the cortex, the neurons were buzzed for about twenty milliseconds, a mere fiftieth of a second. It was enough to evoke a muscle twitch.

No animal ever produced meaningful behavior on a timescale of a fiftieth of a second. But the scientists who studied the motor cortex had plausible reasons for using such blindingly brief stimulation. Their concept of the motor cortex, as I noted earlier, was something like a marionette. If you stimulated a spot in the cortex with the most microscopic amount of stimulation possible—the smallest current and the shortest duration—the activity might behave itself, passing down just one of the marionette strings and reaching the muscles in one location on the body, very possibly even just one single muscle. That was the goal of the stimulation protocol—to map which point in cortex connected to which muscle.

However, the anatomy of the brain conspired against that goal. A typical neuron in the motor cortex may send a connecting strand down to the spinal cord to influence the muscles, but it may also connect to a halo of other neurons around the brain: neurons scattered around the motor cortex, in other far-flung areas of the cerebral cortex, and in structures deep in the brainstem beneath the cortex. The motor control system is more of an interconnected network than a one-way path from point A in the motor cortex to point B in the muscles.

Scientists used weaker and weaker currents, shorter and shorter durations, hoping somehow to prevent the signal from ramifying inconveniently among all the network connections. The hope was that a tiny whisper of a signal would somehow remain confined to the pathway that everyone assumed to be the most important, the descending wire from the cortex to the muscles. If you gave the stimulation too much oomph, the signal might derail off that pathway and spread through the rest of the network.

In effect, scientists treated the widespread connections of the motor cortex as a kind of annoying experimental artifact because it didn't suit the prevailing concept of how the motor system worked.

Occasionally researchers did try longer stimulation.[19-22] But when it was used, it often hinted at a complexity nobody wanted to think about. Complex movements versus twitches? The map of muscle twitches was so well established, so conceptually simple, and had such a hold on the scientific culture, that any complexity lurking under the surface was like Godzilla hunkering under the surface of the ocean. Something horrible, nightmarish, and revolting was threatening an orderly universe.

Different specialties in science tend to develop different traditions. That cultural diversity is a fascinating part of the social construction of science. Scientists who studied the motor cortex had convinced themselves to stick to brief bursts of stimulation. At the same time, a different group of scientists, studying a brain region only a few millimeters away from the motor cortex, developed a totally different concept and a different tradition. When studying the frontal eye field, researchers soon realized that this brain area is only one part of a complex network with a rich connectivity from neuron to neuron and brain area to brain area. In that concept, if you electrically stimulate the frontal eye field, you tickle neurons around the electrode, those neurons spread their activity to many other connected neurons, and an entire functioning network around the brain is rapidly recruited. The artificially injected signal drives the network into a state, and that complex state of the network ultimately drives an eye movement. In that tradition, there was never any question of trying very brief or very weak stimulation in the hope of channeling the signal down one pathway. The activity was obviously going to spread through the entire eye-movement network. If you wanted to evoke a meaningful behavior from the network, such as a coordinated shift in gaze direction instead of a mere eye twitch, you obviously needed to stimulate the network on the timescale of the natural behavior.[4,7,23-26] For an eye movement, that meant anywhere from a tenth to half of a second. That may not sound like a lot, but it is five to twenty times longer than the stimulation typically applied to the motor cortex.

Tirin Moore, studying the frontal eye field and steeped in the traditions of his brain area, had dialed in a half-second of electrical stimulation. But on that one fateful morning, he had gotten his eye-movement protocol into the motor cortex. It was that absurdly tiny mix-up in the protocol, that half-second applied to the motor cortex, that made all the difference. It was why we saw a coherent reach evolve during the stimulation, instead of the traditional arm twitch.

I remember a TV commercial for Reese's Peanut Butter Cups. Two people stumble into each other and one of them says, "Hey, you got your peanut butter in my chocolate!"

We launched a long-term experiment to find out what kinds of complex movement might unfold from the motor cortex during the longer, half-second electrical stimulation.[27] Four of us participated: Tirin Moore, Charlotte Taylor, who was a brilliant graduate student in the lab at that time, the monkey, and me. The monkey was the only one relaxed. He got over his worries. Even though his arms and legs did odd things at which the experimenters cheered, he was happy as long as the raisins and mini-marshmallows kept on coming. We bribed him, is what I am saying.

It was only the fifth day of our new experiment. We pressed the button that triggered a half-second of stimulation to a specific site in the motor cortex. Immediately the monkey closed his hand, pressing the ball of his thumb against the side of his index finger in a typical precision grip for a monkey. He rotated his wrist and forearm to orient the grip toward his mouth. He lifted the hand to his mouth, so that the point of the grip came precisely to the front of the mouth. And he opened his mouth. All of these actions occurred simultaneously, smoothly, so that they looked perfectly spontaneous. The monkey was feeding a bit of empty air to himself. As soon as the stimulation ended, his mouth closed and his hand dropped back down to his lap.

The action could have been a coincidence. Maybe he just felt like picking at his lip at that moment. We could not believe we had triggered it. It was just too ridiculous. We stimulated him a dozen times before we had to accept it. Every stimulation triggered the same movement.

I think the technical term is *mind freak*. I'm not sure how else to describe that moment. Nothing in the brain was supposed to behave in that manner.

We ran out and fetched someone else who happened to be in the building that morning. We wanted him to take a look and make sure we weren't crazy. Well, we pressed the button a few times, the monkey put his hand to his mouth each time, and our casual external observer shrugged and said, "So? I don't get it." He didn't realize that we were causing the movement. It was so natural, so organic, that as far as he could tell, he was watching a monkey chilling and doing monkey things. So we gave him the button and said, "Okay, *you* press." I seem to remember him swearing in shock. If hair ever stood straight up on end in surprise, it happened then. It was a spooky thing to wield that kind of power.

We studied that stimulation site in the brain for hours that day, trying every variation that crossed our minds. We'd entice the monkey with a raisin, luring him to reach to the right, to the left, up, down—it didn't matter. Wherever the monkey's hand started out, the stimulation would instantly drive it directly to the mouth. If the hand was already at the mouth, stimulation just kept it there for half a second with the mouth open.

Just to push the limits of the movement, we let the monkey reach out toward a raisin first. Before he could grasp it, we pressed the stimulation button. His hand instantly closed on empty air an inch shy of the raisin, flipped to aim the grip toward himself, and moved straight back to his mouth. For half a second, the monkey stared at the raisin indignantly with his hand stuck at his mouth and his mouth stuck open. When the stimulation was over, his hand darted back out and greedily snatched at the treat that he had been denied. We didn't try that trick too many times because we didn't want to annoy the monkey.

We reduced the duration. We tried stimulating for a more traditional timescale of twenty milliseconds, and we evoked a twitch. It looked just like the classical descriptions. The fingers twitched. The arm twitched. The lip twitched. When we increased the duration to one hundred milliseconds, more of the movement unfolded. The fingers closed almost all the way, the hand lifted up a few centimeters. When we returned the stimulation to five hundred milliseconds, half a second, we saw the full hand-to-mouth movement unfold. We tried a longer version, a full second of stimulation, but no additional complexity unfolded. The hand came to the mouth and then hovered there, with the mouth open, until the stimulation ended and the monkey was released from that posture.

We put a lead bracelet on the monkey's arm and the stimulation overcame the extra weight and still drove the hand to the mouth.

We did find some limits to the complexity and adaptability of the movement. We put a hard plastic sheet between the hand and the mouth. When we stimulated, the hand did not go intelligently around the obstacle. Instead it followed a straight line toward the mouth, encountered the shield, and remained pressed against it until the end of the stimulation.

The movement was a strange combination of complexity and mechanical stupidity. It had nothing to do with the monkey's own intentions. In later experiments we found that we could anesthetize the monkey and evoke the same movements. We had triggered a fixed motor program that linked together the muscles of the hand, arm, and mouth into a common and useful action.

I used to wonder what it felt like to the monkey to have his limbs move around outside of his control. Since those initial experiments, I've experienced it myself.

There's a method of stimulating the motor cortex in a human volunteer. It's called *transcranial magnetic stimulation* and involves an intense magnetic pulse transmitted directly through the skull. It's one of the mainstays of modern neuroscience. The precision is rather less than in our stimulation experiments in the monkey, however. Instead of stimulating a spot in the cortex the size of a period or smaller, the effect is blunted through the skull and is more like a hammer hitting a nickel-sized area of cortex. You're more likely to get a scrambled mixture than any single coherent action. But it will definitely cause your arm to twitch.

It doesn't hurt, although the magnetic pulse feels a little weird on your scalp. It doesn't even feel like someone else moved your arm. The darn thing just moves. You tend to think that you did it yourself. I was participating in a friend's experiment and was told to relax and sit quietly. Well, my arm moved, so I apologized for being restless. The experimenter snickered and said, "Don't worry, Mike, I did that."

I think this is why the monkeys took to the experiment so well. The actions of their limbs, though a little peculiar, did not much bother them, and at the same time they were rewarded with food and company.

We did the experiment every morning at eight o'clock, often seven days a week, with our coffee or Coca-Cola or whatever stimulant suited each of us. We fetched the monkey from the home colony, at the same time getting a quick look at the morning news on the TV that had been placed in there to entertain them. Then we set up the monkey in the experiment room and picked a spot in the motor cortex to study. We lowered the electrode gently, micron by micron, monitoring the signals like a submarine operator sounding the depth and descending into the darkness. When we heard the crackling of many neurons around the electrode tip, we'd park the electrode and study that cortical site. We were not focused on one neuron at a time as in our previous experiments. Instead, we were studying the whole cluster of neurons surrounding the electrode tip, hundreds or thousands of them in a volume perhaps half a millimeter wide, all sharing similar properties. This clustering of properties is typical of cortical organization. The cluster is called a *cortical column*. The set of neurons packed together in a single column are densely interconnected and process similar information.

That clustering allowed the electrical stimulation method to work. We'd switch the wires so that, instead of measuring brain activity, we could inject current down the electrode into the brain. That current would drive the local cluster of neurons. If each neuron did something different, the result would be a chaos of conflicting signals. But because neurons with similar properties were clumped together, the electrical stimulation tended to excite a small, coherent population and produce an interpretable result.

The current we injected through the electrode was in the form of a square wave pulse. First the current would deflect toward the negative, then toward the positive, then back to neutral. It was the negative deflection that triggered activity in the nearby neurons. The positive deflection was a practical precaution. The pulse was carefully balanced to eliminate any net charge building up that might otherwise damage the neurons. In our experiments, one person was always on duty monitoring the current to make sure that the pulse was still balanced. Each pulse was extremely brief: 0.4 milliseconds. It also carried almost no current: about fifty microamps. Unlike the original experiment by Fritsch and Hitzig in the nineteenth century, if you were to stimulate yourself on the tongue with our parameters you would feel nothing. (I actually tried stimulating myself on the tongue and could not feel the current.) But it was enough to drive the neurons immediately around the electrode tip in a surgically precise manner.

To buzz the neurons and generate a strong signal from that site in the brain, we would set the equipment to repeat at a rate of two hundred pulses per second, the entire train of pulses lasting half a second. Monkeys are fast creatures, their actions like a movie that's been speeded up, and it turns out that half a second is roughly the timescale over which they reach, grasp, and perform other movements of the limbs and mouth.

Finally, once everything was carefully prepared—the equipment set to inject current, the dials on the equipment adjusted to perfection—we would sit in front of the monkey like a panel of judges. One of us held the button that triggered the stimulation, another held a notebook, a third held raisins to treat the monkey, and we'd study the site for hours.

Different spots in the motor cortex triggered different movements. We realized that we were dialing up the monkey's natural repertoire. Reaching, grasping, bringing his hand to the mouth as if feeding, moving all four limbs as if climbing or leaping—we saw the whole repertoire of the monkey acted out in front of us and also spread out as a map on the surface of the brain.

It's difficult to explain the strangeness, the pure astonishment that we felt at pressing a button and triggering a pantomime movement with mechanical reliability, then moving the electrode to a different spot in the cortex and triggering a different, equally complex, equally recognizable action. Nothing like it should have been possible.

Figure 7.2 shows a cartoon summary of the results from many years of experiments.[28-37] The most common, characteristic actions in the monkey's repertoire were laid out in zones on the motor cortex. These broad categories pretty well matched the monkey's natural behavior, as we found when we took a video camera to the zoo and to an island of wild monkeys.

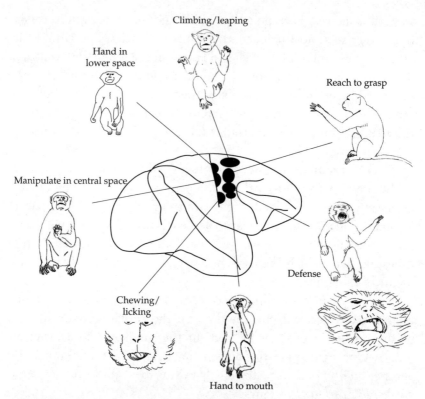

FIGURE 7.2 Action zones in the motor cortex of the monkey. Seven categories of movement that were commonly evoked when the cortex was electrically stimulated on an extended, behaviorally relevant timescale. (Adapted from Graziano [2008].[16])

Our map of actions was initially controversial. Researchers in the motor cortex field did not want to believe anything we had found, and I understand their horror. Exceptional claims require exceptional evidence. As a scientist I subscribe to that adage. Here was something so new, so contrary to the past one hundred thirty years of tradition, that it was almost inconceivable. And yet, there it was. When I gave scientific talks I sometimes felt like an explorer in a pith helmet describing a fabulous world we had discovered in the jungle. To the skeptical audience I could only say, if you don't believe the data I brought back, go see for yourselves. And bit by bit, people did. They tried it for themselves.

By now, fifteen years later, the work is widely accepted. I can't claim one hundred percent acceptance. A few traditionalists remain as holdouts. But every year, neuroscientists publish more and more on the maps of complex actions in monkeys, shrews, rats, mice, cats, squirrels, and humans.[38-57] The picture of the motor cortex has been radically redrawn.[58]

Why did so many previous scientists see a map of the muscles rather than a map of actions? How did the motor homunculus become iconic, if it's so wrong?

The answer is that the homunculus is not wrong. To the extent that the normal movement repertoire can be separated into body parts— chewing is done by the mouth, and grasping by the hand—the map of movements in the brain is arranged as a map of body parts. However, to the extent that the body parts interact—the mouth and the hand often work together, the arm and the leg often coordinate—the map incorporates an overlap of body parts. The cortex does indeed contain a map of the body—a blurry map, a partly overlapping map—just as everyone had described for one hundred thirty years. The homunculus, as far as it goes, is correct, but it misses a deeper organizing principle. The cortex contains a map of the movement repertoire—of the complex interactions among body parts and muscles. Once you understand the movement repertoire, you can understand the cortical map in great detail.[16,35,36]

Chapter 8

Super-Flinchers
and Nerves of Steel

W HAT HAPPENS WHEN YOU ELECTRICALLY STIMULATE
the peripersonal neurons? I had spent years studying those
neurons and wondering about their contribution to behavior. Did
they control reaching? Were they more like a general radar, keeping track of nearby space for any and all purposes? Why were those
sensory neurons in the motor cortex? Now we had a way to ask the
neurons directly.

We lowered an electrode into that polysensory zone in the middle
of the motor cortex and found a cortical site buzzing with peripersonal neurons. At one site, for example, the neurons responded to
touching the left cheek and to the sight of objects looming near the
left side of the face. Then we electrically stimulated the site, revving
up the neurons around the electrode tip. The following set of actions
occurred, all simultaneously.[1]

First, the eyes closed.

Second, the muscles surrounding the eyes contracted, pursing the
skin around the eyes.

Third, the muscles in the cheeks contracted, pulling the upper lip
up, contributing to the protection of the eyes in folds of skin. This
mobilization of the upper lip was especially pronounced on the left
side, exposing the left upper teeth.

Fourth, the monkey's left ear folded back against the head, as though to protect the vulnerable earlobe.

Fifth, the head pulled sharply down and toward the right.

Sixth, the left shoulder shrugged, as though providing some blocking protection to the left side of the neck and face.

Seventh, the left arm lifted in a sharp, fast movement, the hand flapping into a position near the left side of the face, as though to block an impending impact or brush away a noxious insect.

Eighth—and this movement took us some time to discover and properly quantify—the eyes sucked back into the head.[2] This retraction also caused the eyes to bounce to the center of gaze in a characteristic, curved motion. That particular, quirky eye movement was especially important because it is totally unknown in normal behavior *except* during a defensive reaction such as a startle.[3]

The behavior was both realistic and yet artificial at the same time. It involved a natural coordination among hand, arm, shoulder, face, and eye. It looked exactly like a normal flinch. Yet its clockwork reliability was slightly unnerving. As soon as the electrical stimulation started, the movement began. As soon as the stimulation ended, the movement abruptly stopped, which was most unlike a natural defensive flinch. If we stimulated for a shorter duration, we evoked only a short fragment of the movement. If we stimulated for a longer duration, the defensive posture would stick, the hand near the side of the face, the face in an extended squint, until the end of the stimulation train. Colleagues have sometimes asked me: Are these evoked movements truly natural, or are they merely unnatural? I'm not sure that question is scientifically meaningful. The answer, in any case, is both. We seemed to have tapped into a natural defensive circuit using an unnatural signal.

The monkey didn't seem to care. It wasn't as if we had caused him a nasty sensation to which he was reacting with a defensive gesture. He had long since gotten used to his limbs engaging in peculiar involuntary movements. He was happily feeding himself with the right hand at the same time that we were triggering defensive actions that involved the left hand. In one experiment, we anesthetized him and found exactly the same result on electrical stimulation, minus his conscious participation.

We tried a different cortical site, this one with a tactile response on the top of the head and a visual response to objects looming down from upper space toward the face. When we electrically stimulated the site, the head bent sharply down and the eyes closed tightly.

We found a cortical site where the neurons responded to touching the left forearm. They also responded to the sight of objects looming into the space near the forearm. I had spent a decade wondering about the function of arm-related peripersonal neurons like this. Did they form the brain's mechanism for reaching? Did the neurons monitor the location of any object near the arm and, when their activity was revved up enough, cause the arm to move toward that object? That had been my going hypothesis for years. Well, we electrically stimulated the site and blew up that elegant hypothesis.

We waited until the monkey's left arm was relaxed, and then we applied the stimulation. The arm did not move forward. It did not reach into the space that was monitored by those neurons. Instead, the arm immediately whipped into a guarding posture, wrapped around the left side of the torso, the hand hidden behind the monkey's back. The withdrawal looked exactly like a normal defensive withdrawal. It looked like something a startled person might do if a snake struck at her hand. Again, the monkey didn't seem to care. He fed himself raisins with one hand while the other hand engaged in a stereotyped defensive reaction.

This kind of result was consistent across many experiments and monkeys. If the spot in the cortex contained peripersonal neurons with sensory responses that were focused on a specific part of the body, then stimulating that spot in the cortex was likely to evoke a movement that seemed to defend the same part of the body.

These results cleared up quite a few mysteries. One that had nagged at me for years involved a previous experiment on peripersonal neurons and reaching movements. An early report[4] had described neurons with a tactile response on the face and a visual response to objects looming toward the face. At least some of those neurons gave a burst of activity as the monkey moved his hand up near his face. The interpretation at the time was that these neurons must be involved in reaching toward objects near the face. Partly inspired by that finding, I had tried an experiment on neurons with a tactile response on the arm and a visual response to objects looming toward the arm. These neurons, however, went silent if the monkey reached toward nearby objects. (I briefly described this experiment toward the end of Chapter 6.) We considered it a failed experiment and never published it. Why the contradiction? Was the first report correct or was our experiment correct? Did these neurons participate in arm movements or not?

The answer now was suddenly obvious. Both findings were right. A neuron that monitored a bubble of space adjacent to the face was involved in protecting the face, including helping to coordinate an upward, blocking movement of the hand *into* that threatened region of space. A neuron that monitored the space around the arm was involved in withdrawing the arm from a threat, not reaching *toward* nearby objects. The electrical stimulation had revealed the specific, protective movements associated with each kind of peripersonal neuron.

In science, you often want more than one technique to arrive at the same answer. It gives you confidence in the result. In one series of experiments, we manipulated sites in the brain by injecting a chemical instead of using electrical stimulation.[5] The chemical, called muscimol, temporarily inhibits neurons. We could measure that inhibition directly. When the electrode was first parked in place, we would hear the crackling and popping of neuronal activity over the speaker. When we slowly injected the muscimol through a fine syringe into that spot in the cortex, the neuronal activity would disappear. The electrode would go silent. If we waited an hour or two, the activity would slowly come back online again as the effect of the chemical wore off.

With those injections of muscimol into the polysensory zone, we created—for lack of a better term—a monkey with nerves of steel.

We tested his natural defensive reactions in a variety of ways. We bought a ping-pong ball gun, but that didn't work well. It didn't make the monkey flinch. He became skilled at catching the balls and crunching them in his mouth. We loomed at the monkey with our hands outspread, but that did not impress him either. He was so used to us, and had such a good rapport with us, that he merely waited for the raisin that he thought was coming his way. Finally, we settled on air puffs. We hooked a tank of compressed air to a set of regulators and nozzles which allowed us to puff his face in a range of different locations. At the same time, we measured the muscle activity in a variety of facial muscles. The air puff was a gentle stimulus, not too annoying, but it evoked just enough of a defensive blink and squint to allow us to do the experiment.

When we dripped muscimol into the polysensory zone on one side of the brain, the monkey no longer flinched, or at least flinched much less, to an air puff on the opposite side of the face. We noticed that he could still move that side of the face. When he chewed or made faces at us, the muscles were as active as before. Resting muscle tone was also not affected. But when puffed on the cheek, his defensive reaction was reduced. In some tests, he did not even blink. He was James Bond, cool in the face of threat. And that is a remarkable effect. Remember, the eye is heavily protected. When we tried the air puff on ourselves, as gentle as the stimulus was, we found it impossible to suppress the defensive blink and squint. That reflex is strong for good reason. And yet with a microscopic, targeted injection of muscimol, we could selectively shut off the defense on one side of the face.

Then we tried another chemical. Bicuculline has the opposite effect as muscimol. It disinhibits the neurons. It releases them from some of the natural mechanisms that keep neuronal activity in check. The neurons become temporarily more easily excited by any input. When we infused bicuculline into the polysensory zone, the pattern reversed.[5] The monkey became a super-flincher; the air puff evoked a massive facial squint and blink. Heck, we didn't even need the air puff. All we needed was to gently move a finger toward the affected side of the face, and the monkey would reflexively produce a sustained defensive reaction, complete with squinting, shrugging, head turning, and arm and hand lifting. The specificity was impressive. Nothing else about the monkey's behavior had changed. Again, he didn't seem to care. He got his raisins. He seemed to have little interest in these extraneous movements. A half-hour later, after the bicuculline had washed out, the neurons and the monkey's reactions went back to normal.

There is nothing like asking a question if you want an answer. We asked, and the peripersonal neurons answered. They were not coding the space near the body for any generic purpose. They were not an engine for all of sensory-motor integration. They formed a protective shield around the body.

Every time we tested a site in the polysensory zone where we could confirm that the neurons were tuned to the personal space on and near the body, the electrical stimulation evoked a defensive reaction. In later experiments[6] we also tested sites in area VIP, a part of the peripersonal network in the parietal lobe (see Figure 5.1). The results were the same. The electrical stimulation triggered a clear defensive movement no matter where we tested in the peripersonal network. Other experimenters have since found similar results.[7–9]

This unequivocal answer from the peripersonal neurons, the total dominance of defensive movements, caused some concern among colleagues. The peripersonal neurons had finally become accepted in the neuroscience community. In the most common interpretation, these neurons monitored the space around the body as an aid in *all* types of movement. Surely we need that kind of near-space information to reach toward objects, grasp objects, kick, nudge, scratch, avoid, flinch, and so on. How could such an obviously useful, general-purpose mechanism turn out to be limited to a simple flinch reflex?

I don't mean that question to be rhetorical. It's so important that I will try to answer it carefully. I think there are two interrelated answers, detailed in the following sections.

How could the peripersonal neurons be limited to a simple flinch reflex, instead of handling more complex actions such as reaching and grasping?

Answer 1: The brain contains other networks that seem to handle targeted actions such as reaching and grasping.

A huge literature has emerged on the brain basis of reaching and grasping. Two brain areas (shown in Figure 8.1), called the *parietal reach region* and the *dorsal premotor cortex*, use visual information to plan a hand path to a target.[10–19] Another pair of brain areas (also shown in Figure 8.1), called the *anterior intraparietal sulcus* and the *premotor area F5*, use visual information to compute how to shape the fingers in order to accurately grasp an item.[20–25] It has always been difficult to understand how the relatively separate network of peripersonal neurons could control reaching and grasping when other networks already seem to solve those particular problems.

Perhaps the brain computes many kinds of sensory space near the body, each emphasizing a different type of action: a space for reaching, a space for grasping, a space for buffering the self against collision, a space for guiding eye movements, a space for guiding

Parietal Reach Region (PRR) ←——————→ Dorsal Premotor Cortex (PMD)

Ventral Intraparietal Area (VIP) ←——————→ Polysensory Zone

Anterior Intraparietal Area (AIP) ←——————→ Area F5

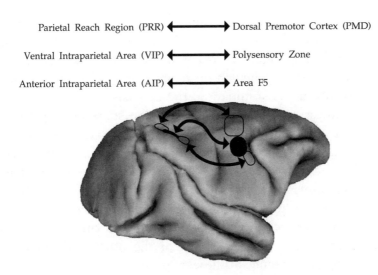

FIGURE 8.1 Areas in the cerebral cortex of the monkey involved in reaching (parietal reach region and dorsal premotor cortex), in protecting a margin of safety (ventral intraparietal area and polysensory zone) and in shaping the hand for grasping (anterior intraparietal area and area F5). Image of monkey cortex provided by Mark Pinsk, Princeton University.

walking or running. No doubt these many types of space interact. The networks in the brain that compute these spaces may engage in some crosstalk, but the different networks appear to emphasize fundamentally different categories of action. This view of multiple spaces represented in the brain, each one tuned to the demands of a specific kind of action, was described particularly clearly by Carol Colby.[26] The peripersonal neurons—the particular neurons that have a tactile response so sensitive that it can be triggered by bending a single hair, and a visual response that is strongest to objects near and looming toward the body—these neurons seem to be tuned specifically to a protective function.

How could the peripersonal neurons be limited to a simple flinch reflex?

Answer 2: It's no simple reflex.

Peripersonal neurons are not flinch neurons. They're more like margin-of-safety neurons. Flinching is a tiny fraction of their complex operating range.

When the peripersonal neurons are revved up at two hundred spikes per second by our intense stimulation, the result is a massive, recognizable defensive reaction. But that is an extreme. It shows the system at one end of its operating range. If we reduce the intensity of the stimulation, the defensive reaction becomes weaker, slower, until at low intensity the stimulation produces no overt behavior at all. We stimulate and the arm lies still. But the stimulation can still warp ongoing behavior. For example, suppose the monkey reaches toward a raisin. In mid-reach, we apply the weak stimulation. The result? The hand no longer moves along the shortest path to the raisin. Instead, the stimulation seems to give it a tiny, deflecting nudge and it follows a curved path. This more subtle effect may be closer to the normal, moment-by-moment operating range of these neurons.

Normally, as we know from our experiments, an object near the body will cause the peripersonal neurons to respond. But the response is not usually a shrill maximum. It might be a gentle response. The neurons might fire a little more rapidly than usual. That low level of activity does not translate into an overt action. It's nowhere near strong enough to trigger a flinch. And a good thing, too, otherwise we would flinch and cringe at every object near us or touching us—a behavioral disaster. Instead, the constant subtle reactions of these neurons to nearby objects presumably cause a subtle adjustment to ongoing behavior. The system nuances how we interact with the world.

By studying human and monkey behavior, I think I've finally come to understand the pervasive and foundational role of the margin of safety. Here are a few examples from everyday life to illustrate what I mean.

At this moment, I'm sitting at my desk. My arms are moving about as I type, reach for the phone, open a drawer, or pick up a pencil that I've dropped on the floor. I could easily bruise my arms against the sharp edge of the desk. It's an unforgiving object. If my arms were moving at their normal peak speed during a reach and came in contact with that edge, I'm sure I'd get a bruise. What's keeping my arms from getting hurt? As if my body had a mind of its own, my arms simply avoid those harmful collisions. The computations are so far under the surface of consciousness that nobody notices just how astonishing that everyday ability is. It's hard to appreciate the relative absence of disasters. We tend to take it for granted and not think too much about our good luck.

Some people are clumsy, but by and large, when you walk through a doorway, you don't bash your shoulder on the doorframe. You don't need to think about it—something is keeping track of the objects around you, even objects outside your focus of attention, and shaping your ongoing behavior to avoid collisions.

A few weeks ago, somebody was standing behind me in the lobby of my office building, raising his rain hood. I didn't hear him because the rain outside was making a racket. My personal space mechanism did not register him. I turned around and bashed my eye on his raised elbow. You don't realize how much force is in back of the simple act of turning around until you hit your face on something unexpectedly. That kind of hard contact is essentially impossible when your personal space system has correctly pegged the locations of the objects near you. That system cushions your movements. It prevents most of those little tragedies. When the system makes a mistake, Pow! That's when you realize how important it is.

For an ambitious three months, a few years back, I attended a weekly karate class. I never got beyond an orange belt. I was not a stellar student. One thing I did learn, however, was that people almost always pull their punches. You can't help it. Something in you protects your fist. One mechanism in your brain is directing your hand to hit that board with full force, but another unconscious mechanism is pulling back, cringing at the last moment. It takes some training to overcome that inner protective impulse. My reason for including this particular example is to emphasize how the margin of safety is not always about withdrawing from threats. It also nuances movements that are directed *toward* objects. A protective mechanism may not specifically guide your hand to the target, but it can protect your hand as it approaches. The margin of safety works in tandem with reaching, grasping, hitting, and other targeted actions.

Recently, I was reaching to pick up a freshly baked chocolate chip cookie. I knew it was hot and my hand did a dance—reaching, shaping, and hesitating. I gingerly picked it up. Again, the margin of safety is not simply a withdrawal mechanism. It operates in tandem with reaching out and grasping. That same cushioning mechanism is presumably applied, in a less obvious way, every time we reach for anything. Otherwise we'd injure our fingers, knock over our drinks, and risk painfully poking people every time we try to tap them on the shoulder.

A friend and I were visiting the Grand Canyon. I had never seen such a deep hole in my life. We started at the top and walked down the trail, which wound back and forth along the steep side of the canyon. It was a narrow, gravelly path with a cliff rising up on one side and a frightful drop falling away on the other. I pointed to a tourist couple walking in front of us and whispered, "Look at them. Look at how they're leaning." The couple looked like somebody had sawed a few inches off one leg. They were leaning heavily away from the dangerous drop to the side. They didn't even seem to know they were doing it. I thought it was funny. But my friend whispered back, "Dude, you're doing the same damn thing yourself." It was true. We were all leaning. Something in us had registered the location of danger and was nuancing our ongoing movements, biasing us away from the danger. To stand upright seemed to require an extra effort, as though I were fighting an invisible force.

Another time, I was disembarking from an airplane. It was one of those smaller airlines that somehow didn't get proper space at the airport terminal. The passengers were herded onto a bus that transported us to the arrival gate. But the bus was too small. The attendants pushed and cajoled until we were smashed on, standing one against the next. I had never been so tightly packed. Not even on the New York subway, not even on New Jersey Transit. I'm pretty sure it violated some safety code. I noticed that nowhere was anyone's face or front of the body touching anyone else. No matter how the space around us was compressed, something psychological pushed back like a spring.

Just a few months ago I was almost hit by a skateboarder. He was practicing a complicated maneuver that involved flinging himself down a set of concrete steps into a courtyard. I was coming up the same steps, muttering parts of a lecture I was preparing to give. At the last instant I looked up and saw the looming blur. Before I even realized what was happening, the key areas in my brain sprang into action and saved me from my own absent-mindedness. I found myself crouching into a half turn, my arms pulling tight around myself. The skateboarder zipped past, missing me by inches as a loose flap of his T-shirt brushed my ear. He landed in a heap on the stone flagging below, his body in a protective curl, the skateboard bouncing off the ground twenty feet away. He seemed okay. He didn't say anything, so I didn't either. Just another Wednesday, I guess. I un-crouched myself and walked on. He collected his skateboard and flung himself down the stairs again.

The margin of safety around the body is foundational. It shapes almost every moment of our lives. It manifests itself in the constant, subtle nuancing of ongoing behavior and occasionally in overt, fast defensive flinches. It's always with us, whether beneath consciousness or intruding into it.

We've come close to understanding how the margin of safety is wired into the brain, at least in broad outline. It's partly a simulated bubble wrap, an invisible second skin surrounding the body that emphasizes nearby space while also weakly representing far space, keeping track of objects through sight, sound, touch, and even memory in the dark. It depends on a well-defined set of brain areas and specialized neurons that have elegant properties. It's been studied in detail in monkeys. In the last fifteen years, an explosion of new research has revealed a similar mechanism in people. The next chapter describes that new wave of research.

Chapter 9

The Peripersonal Radar
in Humans

W E HUMANS RESEMBLE MONKEYS MORE THAN I CARE
to admit. Neuroscientists have traditionally taken advantage
of that similarity, studying brain mechanisms in monkeys and then
extrapolating the findings to humans. In the past several chapters,
I described twenty years of experiments on monkeys that revealed
the outlines of a network in the brain for monitoring a margin of
safety around the body. Although the human brain is about ten times
larger than a monkey's and the cortex contains many more functional areas, especially related to higher cognition and language, it's
likely to have a similar peripersonal network. A system as basic for
survival as monitoring and defending personal space is likely to be
retained. It may, however, have its own human quirks and modifica-
tions, perhaps related to tool use or social interaction.

But testing the human brain is a challenge. The most direct
methods are possible but rarely used. For example, much of what
I described in the previous chapters depended on lowering electrodes
into the brain and measuring the activity of individual neurons. This
approach, spying on the brain's logic gates, is simple and powerful.
It's sometimes done in human patients who are outfitted with electrodes for medical reasons, but it's rare. I don't know of any such
experiments in the human brain on peripersonal neurons.

Electrical stimulation, pumping artificial signals down the electrode and into clusters of neurons, led to incredible insights when applied to the monkey brain. This method also has a long history in humans, but again depends on patients whose brains are being probed for clinical reasons. As an experimenter, you don't have much choice of brain area to study. I don't know of any stimulation experiments on human peripersonal neurons.

Lacking the most direct methods, researchers must rely on cleverness to get at the problem from unexpected angles. In the past fifteen years, scientists have risen to that challenge magnificently. Experiments of amazing cleverness have probed the peripersonal space in humans, taking advantage of subtle quirks in our behavior to reveal what may be going on inside the brain.

I need to make two qualifications at the outset of this chapter.

First, when scientists study the space near the body by closely examining human behavior, they are not tapping into a pure signal. They are likely to see the combined effects of many brain systems, not just the peripersonal neurons that code for a margin of safety. Other systems in the brain may emphasize space for reaching, for grasping, for moving the eyes, or for walking. All of these systems are active at the same time, and their quirks come through in the details of human action. In many of the experiments I'll describe in this chapter, it is difficult or impossible to separate out these many different influences.

Second, because peripersonal space interacts with so much of our normal behavior, the relevant literature is almost unending. Every year, more and more experiments show evidence of the special treatment of the space near the body and its involvement in almost every part of daily life. Rather than try to review everything and turn this chapter into a hefty book unto itself, I'll give examples of a few experiments that strike me as especially clever and insightful. My apologies to those who have done excellent experiments not represented here.

Neglect, Near and Far

Imagine waking up in the hospital with the left half of space erased from your consciousness. You don't even know what you're missing. Everyone else around you can see and react to things that are outside your own comprehension. The syndrome is called *hemispatial neglect* and it is one of the most bizarre and horrible syndromes caused by brain damage.[1-4] It's often caused by stroke damage to the right side of the cerebral cortex, at the junction between the parietal lobe and the temporal lobe.[5,6] The patient loses awareness of the left half of space. Although the sides can be reversed, with left brain damage causing right neglect, that version is more rare, for reasons that are still debated.

The patient might talk to people standing to the right side of his bed and ignore those standing to the left. He might eat the food on the right side of his plate and assume that he's done. When somebody rotates the plate, he wonders where that extra food came from. He might dress only one side of his body. It doesn't occur to him that he has a left arm or that his shirt has a left sleeve. The problem even extends to his imagination. If you ask him to imagine standing in a familiar city square,[7] he'll describe from memory only the buildings on the right, not the left. If you ask him to imagine standing on the opposite side of the same city square, he'll remember the opposite set of buildings, and forget the first set. If you ask him to draw a clock face, he'll draw a circle and then crush all the numbers, one through twelve, along the right side.[8] Evidently he knows he needs to put in twelve numbers, but he can no longer conceptualize the left half of space. The patients often know that they're giving contradictory or nonsensical answers, and it can distress them. But they can't figure out where they made the mistake because they can no longer even imagine the left side of space. This crippling spatial confusion can last for months and in some patients for years.

Neglect is often measured with a quick, simple test that requires no complicated equipment and therefore can be done in a hospital setting. The patient is given a piece of paper with a horizontal line on it and told to draw a tic mark through the center point of the line. A normal person can bisect the line quite accurately. The patient with neglect fails to process the left side of the line and therefore draws the tic mark far to the right of center.[9]

But the symptoms are not always straightforward. Sometimes buried in them you can find bizarre contradictions. Take the same patient who could not bisect a line on a sheet of paper and sit him in front of a wall that's just out of reach. Draw a horizontal line on the wall and ask him to bisect it with a laser pointer.[10] That same patient may be able to perform quite well. Near space, not so much. Far space, no problem.

This kind of experiment[10–21] confirms that the brain breaks space into at least two different parts: the space of things you can reach and the space too far away to reach. (In the next chapter I'll discuss what happens when reachable space is extended by a handheld tool.) It seems that in some patients, the peripersonal machinery is damaged while sparing the machinery for more distant space. Other patients show the opposite pattern.[11,13–15] They can process nearby locations but fail at distant space. It's always spooky when brain damage takes away specific pieces of the mind.

Extinction

As a neglect patient slowly recovers, the symptoms often fade into a less severe form of the disease called *extinction*.[22] If a single picture is presented on a screen, the patient will be able to see it. Present the picture anywhere, up or down, on the left or right side of space, and the patient can point to it and tell you about it. It looks as though the patient has recovered from the neglect syndrome. But if two pictures are presented at the same time, one on the left and one on the right, the right one will capture the patient's attention and effectively extinguish the left one. The neglect returns and the patient reports only the picture on the right.

Elisabetta Làdavas and her colleagues used the phenomenon of extinction to perform a series of clever experiments.[23–32] These experiments depended on stripping down the sensory input to a bare minimum—spots of light and touches on the hand. The experimenters focused on patients who suffered from a special kind of extinction that affected their perception of touch, rather than vision. The patient sat at a table with both hands resting in view on the tabletop. A mechanical device gently touched one hand or the other. The patient could report the touch. But if both hands were touched at the same time, the patient reported only the touch on the right hand, neglecting the touch on the left. The patient suffered from extinction in the tactile domain.

Next, the experimenters tried mixing touch and vision. Would a visual stimulus near the right hand extinguish the patient's ability to feel a touch on the left hand? A small light was turned on near the right hand at the same time that a touch was delivered to the left hand. Again, the patient failed to notice the touch. Vision and touch seemed to be fused together. An event on one side, whether it was felt or seen, wiped out the patient's ability to detect a touch on the other side.

Finally, the experimenters tried changing the distance between the light and the hand. It turned out that when the light was far away from the right hand, it no longer extinguished the patient's processing around the left hand. It was as if the right hand had a restricted bubble of space around it, glued to it, moving as the arm moved. Anything in that bubble, whether seen or felt, had an impact, extinguishing the perception of events on the left hand.

That sphere of influence around the hand sounds a lot like the properties of the peripersonal neurons that my lab described in the monkey brain.[33] Many of the peripersonal neurons had a tactile response on the hand and a visual response to objects near the hand. When the hand was moved, the visually responsive region moved with it like a balloon surrounding the hand.

Làdavas and her colleagues used their extinction method in a series of experiments to show that people also have a bubble of space around the face and around the torso.[25,32] These bubbles of space are sensitive to touch, to vision, and to sounds.[28,29] Humans apparently have a peripersonal mechanism much like monkeys do. It monitors the space around the body by combining the senses, and the crucial region of space clings to the body surface, warping and changing as the head and the limbs move. That mechanism is partially damaged in at least some patients, and careful experiments on those patients can reveal an echo of the underlying spatial computations.

Cross-Cuing

The studies I've described so far in this chapter involve brain damage. As tragic as it is at a personal level, brain damage gives science a guilty glimpse into how the brain works. The healthy brain gives the impression of a single, seamless intelligence. When specific regions are damaged, the seams begin to show. Functions begin to break apart—like near space and far space—and we begin to learn about the underlying mechanisms. But nature doesn't conduct clean experiments. A stroke can cause large, messy damage that sprawls across many networks in the cortex and causes a confusing mixture of symptoms. Adding to the complexity, after the damage occurs the brain starts to re-wire, developing abnormal compensations and workarounds. When you study brain-damaged patients, how much of the insight can be extrapolated to the normal, undamaged brain? Probably a lot, but probably not all. For these reasons, it's important to confirm the findings in the normal population, in volunteers with no brain damage or abnormality.

You need to be especially clever to study brain function in normal volunteers. You're looking for the subtlest of signs in human behavior that hint at the wheels and gears working under the surface. One experimental paradigm, sometimes called *cross-cuing*, has become the workhorse of this corner of the literature, probing how the brain processes nearby space. It's not the only available paradigm, but it's simple, easy to do with minimal cost, and, even more importantly, easy to modify so that it can address the issue of nearby space from many different angles.

Cross-cuing was developed by John Driver and Charles Spence, beginning in 1998.[34–39] The paradigm has many versions. In one simple version, if you're a volunteer, you sit at a table with both arms on the tabletop. Your index finger is pressed into a mechanical device that can deliver a brief, gentle vibration. Your task is to report as quickly as possible whether the vibration is continuous or pulsed. It's not a difficult task. Every few seconds a new stimulus is applied to your finger and you respond. Sometimes the right hand is stimulated, sometimes the left—the task is the same in either case.

At the same time, other stimuli are presented around you. A small light might flash near your right hand or near your left. The light has nothing to do with your task. Your best bet is to ignore it, but it has an impact on your responses nevertheless. If the light flashes on your right side and immediately afterward the vibration is applied to your right index finger, you're involuntarily faster to respond to the vibration. It's as if the light draws your attention to the space around your hand, allowing you to process the touch on your hand more quickly. Likewise, if the light flashes near your *left* hand and immediately afterward the vibration is applied to your *right* index finger, you're slower to respond to the vibration. Evidently, the light temporarily drew your attention to the space around your left hand and away from your right hand.

By presenting that light in different places with respect to the hand, and also placing the hand in different locations, the experimenters were able to map out the critical region of space surrounding the hand in which the light affected the processing of touch on the hand. The result was consistent with a bubble of space anchored to the hand, a lot like the responsive area of a peripersonal neuron.

This result became known as the cross-modal congruency effect, or cross-cuing. Many experiments have since confirmed that people have a subtle benefit to processing stimuli near the skin, whether those stimuli are visual or auditory, and whether they are near the hand, the arm, the face, the trunk, or generally near the whole body.[40-54] The human brain apparently constructs a shell of visual and sonic space around the self. The experiment can even be done without the cross-cuing at all, using a single stimulus such as a spot of light. Just ask the volunteer to react to the spot of light, and the reaction time is faster when the light happens to be presented near the volunteer's hand.[48,49]

To me, the incredible value of these studies is that, without ever putting an electrode in a person's head, researchers can probe the quirks and specifics of how the brain processes the space near the body. The cross-cuing experiments, the experiments on extinction, and the experiments on hemispatial neglect all converge on the same answer. The space immediately around the body has special representation in the brain. The senses are welded together into a visual–auditory–tactile radar for nearby objects. And it isn't just one radar system. There is no single giant bubble of space around the body. Instead, each body part seems to have its own bubble surrounding it. The mechanism, therefore, does not keep track of the locations of objects from a single point of reference on the head or the chest, as in more classical theories of spatial processing. Instead, it uses what I originally termed "body-part-centered coordinates,"[55] a flexible spatial construction that monitors space with respect to many reference points distributed over the body. It's as though, rather than living in our own personal army tank built around the body, each of us is living inside a suit of articulated, medieval armor that bends as the limbs and head move.

The Margin of Safety

The experiments that I just described involve simple, boring visual stimuli, like spots of light. What happens if you replace the spots with something more interesting, like a spider? One cross-cuing experiment found that people could detect a touch on the hand better and faster if a spider was looming toward the hand than if an innocent butterfly was looming toward the hand.[56] The result is reminiscent of our biblical neurons that responded like crazy to an approaching rubber snake and fell silent to an approaching apple.[57] It suggests that the peripersonal mechanism in humans, like in monkeys, emphasizes protecting the body.

The hand blink reflex, studied by Iannetti and his colleagues, is one of my favorite examples of protective space in humans.[58–63] It's a simple paradigm. A mild shock is applied to your hand. If your hand is near your face, you blink. If your hand is far from your face, you don't blink. By placing the hand in many different locations, the experimenters could map the protective border around the face. The method revealed an invisible shell around the head much like the receptive fields of peripersonal neurons.

Another of my favorite examples involves reaching while avoiding an obstacle. We automatically curve our hand path around the obstacle.[64–66] Even if the distracting object isn't in the way, if it's anywhere nearby it seems to "push" on the hand and nudge the path of the reach out of a straight line into a curve. In one particularly simple study,[66] people reached toward a target while a glass of water stood nearby. The path of the hand was distorted as though the glass exerted a repulsive force field. That distortion depended on whether the glass was empty and therefore not much of a risk, or full and therefore more worthy of caution. I like this example because it tests a simple, everyday phenomenon. Almost every reach we make happens in a cluttered environment. Whether we realize it explicitly or not, we're constantly monitoring and adjusting to make sure no part of the arm or hand collides with anything it shouldn't.

My point is not that the brain monitors the space near the body *solely* for self-protection. I don't want to shoehorn all the near-space data into the category of defense. As I noted in Chapter 8, the brain probably constructs many different representations of space for purposes of reaching, grasping, and other everyday actions. But there is something special about the peripersonal mechanism with its bubbles of space anchored to the limbs and the head. That particular mechanism, encoding nearby space in that particular geometric style, seems to emphasize self-protection.

Feathered Hats and Rubber Hands

A woman with a tall ostrich feather in her hat ducks into a covered, horse-drawn carriage without breaking the feather. How does she do it?

In 1911, the British neurologists Sir Henry Head and Sir Gordon Holmes asked that seemingly trivial question. Buried in the middle of a massive treatise on brain-damaged patients,[67] they mused about the special skill of wearing a feathered hat. To answer the question, the two researchers floated what turned out to be one of the most important and enduring ideas in psychology and neuroscience. That one speculative paragraph had more of an impact on science than the rest of the book-length manuscript.

They proposed that the brain constructs a body schema (or "postural schema" as they called it). The body schema is a simulation. It's a computed set of information about the shape and structure of the body. It keeps track of your limbs, torso, and head—their size and shape, how they're hinged together, where they are at any moment, and how they're moving.[67-71] The body schema supplies your understanding of who you are as a physical being. It allows the brain to accurately plan and adjust movement. According to Head and Holmes, the women who were so expert at wearing a feathered hat must have incorporated the feather into the body schema. At an unconscious level, the feather was processed like an extension of the body with a normal margin of safety wrapped around it. It was as though the women had simply grown an exceptionally tall head for the evening. And it makes sense that the body schema should be so easily adaptable. As you grow up, your body changes in size and shape, and the body schema must keep up with those changes.

Feathered hats are now a little out of date. My favorite modern demonstration of the body schema is the rubber-hand illusion, studied by Matthew Botvinick and Jonathan Cohen in 1998.[72] It's a spooky illusion easy to inflict on a friend, or for a friend to inflict on you.

You sit with one arm (let's say your right arm) resting on a table. The arm is blocked from your view with a piece of cardboard. Also resting on the table, in plain view, is a fake rubber hand. A glove will do in a pinch, or take a trip to a Halloween store and invest in a quality rubber hand. For an extra touch of realism you can arrange a sleeve connecting the rubber hand to your shoulder. Even with a sleeve, the fake hand doesn't look particularly convincing and certainly won't fool you. When I've given a try at testing the rubber-hand illusion on students, I find that the students often giggle at the absurdity.

Your friend, sitting across the table from you, holds two small paintbrushes. With one brush, she gently strokes your real hand. With the other brush, she strokes the rubber hand. From your point of view, you can't see her touching your real hand, though obviously you can feel it. You can see only the stroking on that rubber hand. Every stroke that you feel on your own hand is accompanied by a stroke that you can see on the fake hand.

After a few minutes of this synchronous stroking, you may experience a spooky sensation. The rubber hand starts to feel like your own hand. Cognitively, you know it isn't. But it somehow attaches itself to you. I've experienced this illusion myself, and it's difficult to put into words just how strong and startling the sensation can be. That rubber thing becomes a part of your body. It's as though an invisible energy, a part of your essence, extends out and invests the rubber hand. Your body schema has incorporated the fake hand.

In the second stage of the demonstration, your friend makes a subtle adjustment, stroking the rubber hand and your real hand asynchronously. The offset is only a fraction of a second, but it's enough to remind your body schema that the touch you feel and the touch you see are not the same. Almost immediately, the illusion disappears. It's just a rubber hand again.

The strength of the illusion can be measured in many ways, but my favorite is to pull out a hammer or a knife and bring it down on the rubber hand.[73] If the illusion is in full swing, you'll give a defensive startle, maybe even yanking your hand into a guarding posture beside your body. Your skin conductance response will shoot up. Since you know the rubber hand is not your own, it's common to laugh or to feel some embarrassment about that involuntary protective reflex. It's a different matter if the illusion is not present, such as during the asynchronous stroking. Then, the hammer smash may be a bit startling, but it doesn't evoke the same reflexes to protect the hand or quite the same level of skin conductance response.

The rubber-hand illusion shows just how close that link is between the body schema and the protective space around the body. To the brain, the peripersonal space is an extension of the body. It's an invisible, squishy, penetrable part of the body surrounding the firmer, visible part. Both belong to you in some fundamental way and both are guarded.

Nobody has pushed our understanding of the rubber-hand illusion more than Henrik Ehrsson and his colleagues at the Karolinska Institute.[74–81] I can't do justice to all the clever, wonderful experiments they have done, but I'll describe a few that are particularly relevant to peripersonal space. In one version of the illusion,[81] the researchers discovered that the paintbrush doesn't actually have to touch the rubber hand. In that variant, the experimenter brushes your real hand out of view with one paintbrush, while at the same time, in view, brushes the empty air a few centimeters *above* the rubber hand with another paintbrush. It's a bizarre manipulation with an unexpected result.

Just as in the standard rubber-hand illusion, you feel as though the rubber hand now belongs to you. It's your hand, in a spooky way. It has become a part of your body. At the same time, you feel as though there's a magnetic force pulling your hand upward, toward the hovering paintbrush. There's no cognitive confusion. You know the rubber hand is a fake and there is no real magnetic force. But the perceptual illusion is powerful. The rubber hand seems to have an invisible force field around it, interacting with the paintbrush.

This magnetic-touch illusion has a spatial limit. If the paintbrush hovers ten centimeters above the rubber hand, the illusion works. If the brush hovers a meter above the rubber hand, the illusion fails. The break is at about forty centimeters. The rubber hand has a bubble of space around it in which touch and vision are able to interact. It's an elegant demonstration of how peripersonal space is partly constructed from the hand outward.

To me, the most bizarre version of the rubber-hand illusion dispenses with the rubber hand altogether. In this version,[79,80] you're lying on the floor with your head propped up on a pillow so that you can see down the length of your body. However, rather than looking directly at your own body, you're wearing video goggles linked to a camera. What you see is the floor of a room with a body lying in a position consistent with your own. It's as though you're looking at your own self, stretched out, with a shirt, jeans, and sneakers. Of course, you're not fooled by the visual image. You know you're being fed a video image from somewhere else. There's no cognitive confusion. It doesn't really look convincingly like your own body anyway.

The experimenters use a stick to gently stroke your stomach. You can feel the stroking. At the same time, they use another stick to make similar, synchronous stroking movements in the field of view of the video camera, on the stomach of the fake body. You *see* a probe stroking the fake body and *feel* the touch on your own body. The result? After a minute or two, you experience the spooky sensation that the fake body belongs to you. It seems like your own. You know it's an illusion, but the perception is strong. These illusions of the body schema lie much deeper than intellectual understanding.

Now the experimenters try a variant of the procedure. Again they stroke your stomach and synchronously stroke a fake body in front of the video camera. This time, however, the fake body is a twelve-foot-tall giant. The result? Again you develop a spooky illusion that you're looking at your own body lying on the floor. But you don't develop the illusion that your body is huge. Your body feels normal sized. Instead, the room around it looks Lilliputian. Your normal-sized body is lying on the floor of a tiny room with tiny furniture crowded around you.

The same procedure works just as well in the opposite direction. The experimenters stroke your stomach. Synchronously, they stroke a fake body in front of the video camera, but the fake body is the size of a Barbie doll. The illusion sets in again. You feel as though you have a normal-sized body that is lying on the floor of a Brobdingnagian room. The walls are far away and the furniture is too large for a normal person to use.

These experiments show that we humans understand the space around us from the body outward. The brain constructs the body schema, our internal model of the body. From that core, the brain then reconstructs the spaces that surround the body.

The Peripersonal Network in the Human Brain

In Chapter 5, I described a network of areas in the monkey brain that processes peripersonal space (see Figure 5.1). Figure 9.1 shows some of the peripersonal network in the human brain, at least as it has been studied so far.[82–92] It includes a region in the parietal lobe that's probably roughly equivalent to the monkey area VIP, and a region in the motor cortex that's probably equivalent to the monkey polysensory zone. I suspect the network is larger. It probably includes other cortical regions and other structures beneath the cortex such as the putamen, but the data are incomplete as yet. Different studies show a mixture of different brain areas, and the ones shown in Figure 9.1 are the most consistent.

One of the myths perpetrated on the general public about neuroscience is that you can stick someone in a functional magnetic resonance imaging (fMRI) scanner, give them a task, and see which

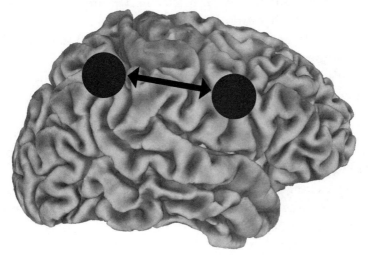

FIGURE 9.1 The peripersonal network in the human brain. Most studies of the processing of peripersonal space in the human brain show centers of activity in the posterior parietal cortex and the ventral premotor cortex. These two cortical regions may correspond to two areas originally discovered in the monkey brain: area VIP in the parietal lobe and the polysensory zone in the motor cortex. The human peripersonal network probably contains many more brain areas, including subcortical structures, but has not yet been fully mapped.

spots in the brain light up. The truth is a bit more complicated. The brain is a constant roil of activity. If you find activity in one location at one time, that by itself is not usually meaningful. Instead, you're always comparing two conditions to determine if a brain region is more active in one condition than in the other. Unless the experiment is thoughtfully designed, the results can be hard to interpret.

For example, in an experiment by Tamar Makin and her colleagues,[84] a volunteer lies in the bed of the scanner and a visual stimulus, a moving ball, looms into the space near the body. In Condition 1, the participant's hand is near the looming ball. In Condition 2, the hand is placed farther from the ball. The visual stimulus is the same, but its proximity to the hand has changed. Of course, much of the brain will respond to the visual stimulus, but do any brain areas respond *more* in Condition 1 than in Condition 2? If so, then those brain areas may contain peripersonal neurons tuned to the space near the hand. This particular experiment reveals that when the hand is near the ball, activity is greater in a range of brain areas including part of the parietal lobe, possibly corresponding to area VIP, and part of the frontal lobe, possibly corresponding to the polysensory zone.

Here's another elegant experiment.[88] A volunteer lies in the scanner. On some trials an air puff stimulates the face. On other trials a visual stimulus looms toward the face. Although many areas scattered around the brain respond with a jump in activity to one or the other stimulus, only a select few brain areas respond to both types of stimuli. One of those combination, multisensory brain areas is again in the parietal lobe, possibly corresponding to area VIP. Another is in the frontal lobe, possibly corresponding to the polysensory zone.

Hapless participants have had a whole miscellany of stuff loom at their faces, hands, and bodies.[82-92] Sometimes the intruding item is a sound source, sometimes a picture of a face, sometimes a ball on a stick. Sometimes the activity of brain areas is measured in an MRI scanner. Sometimes magnetic pulses are passed through the skull to temporarily disrupt a brain area, while people's responses are measured. Throughout all these manipulations, the two brain areas most consistently related to peripersonal space are a region in the parietal lobe that may match area VIP and a region in the frontal cortex that may match the polysensory zone.

By now at least the rough outlines of the peripersonal network have been confirmed in monkeys and in humans. It has been measured and tested in dozens of ways. The methods have ranged from monitoring the activity of single neurons, to applying direct stimulation of the brain, to taking measurements in brain-damaged people, to observing the subtleties of our reactions to lights, sounds, and touches. This accumulation of science is a rare and beautiful example of the convergence of evidence. Not many stories in neuroscience have so many pieces that fit together so well. And the science is only just beginning. We can expect a flood of experiments in the coming years probing the peripersonal network, disrupting it, activating it, and measuring how it lights up under many different conditions.

And yet, despite all of that foundational work on peripersonal space, I have not even begun to describe the most interesting part of the story. Now that we have a handle on the brain machinery, we can ask much more profound questions that should interest everyone. How does the peripersonal machine impact the rest of our lives? How does it affect our sense of self, our ability to use tools, our culture, and our social and emotional behavior? It turns out that operating in the background, mostly unconsciously, the peripersonal mechanism has had an outsized influence on what it means to be human. The remaining chapters focus on these larger questions.

Chapter 10

Wrapping Personal Space
Around My Black & Decker

I MAGINE YOU'RE A *HOMO HABILIS* TWO MILLION YEARS AGO, in the Olduvai Gorge in Africa. You're sitting on the dusty ground in the sun, making a stone tool. You pick up a large core of flint about the size of a football and rest it on your knee, stabilizing it with your left hand. Then you take a smaller hammer stone in your right hand and strike near the edge of the core. The blow knocks off sharp flakes from the underside of the core. The raw flakes may do well by themselves as knives. You can slice a piece of meat with no trouble. You can also shape the flakes further if you like, tapping them, rubbing them, striking here and there with the hammer stone. This is the basic method of flint knapping used by our ancestors for millions of years, starting when their brains were only a third the size of ours.[1-4]

Modern paleoanthropologists have reconstructed how stone tools were made at different stages in our history, from simple flake technology to much more complex technology that produced beautifully contoured and fluted spear and arrow heads.[1-4] All of our awesome and sometimes frightening human technology, from architecture to computers, from automobiles to space flight, sprang ultimately from that original stone tool capability.

Our ancestors must have had a special kind of intelligence. Stone knapping is an art. It isn't enough to bash one stone against another, although maybe that's how the skill began. You have to learn the subtle relationship between where you strike the core, how hard, at what angle, and what shape of flake will come off the other side. You have to learn what kinds of rocks make good material and what kinds don't. Even if you have the right kind of rock, you have to recognize whether the core is a quality one or has disqualifying seams or faults. It helps to have a vivid imagination so that you can picture how you'll use the tool and therefore what specific shape it ought to have. Once you've made the tool, you need the finger strength, complex grip, and dexterity to hold it. You need good visually guided aiming to use it. All of these capabilities had to evolve and merge together for our ancestors to develop tools.

But I'd like to direct attention to another, even more fundamental ability that you must have to use a stone tool. That ability is usually hidden. We tend not to think of it as a part of tool use—in fact, we tend not to think about it at all—but without it our ancestors would not have gotten their fledgling tool industry off the ground.

We extend our peripersonal buffer zone around the tool.

When you hold the core in your left hand on your knee and strike it with the hammer stone in your right hand, it's distressingly easy to skin your left hand or bruise your knee. I know, because I've tried. Making a stone tool is an educational exercise that everyone should try at some point. It's a return to our most distant roots. You have to be aware at all times of the space around the hammer stone. When you swing it, you don't want to hit your knee, your fingers, or, for that matter, the bridge of your nose on the upswing, especially if you're hunched intently over the task. You must monitor the space around all parts of that hammer at all times, keeping track of the potential for collision.

Once you've fashioned your stone cutter—which, by the way, can have an edge as sharp as a surgeon's scalpel—you need to be mighty careful where you swing it. Using a knife is not just a matter of aiming the blade at the desired target. You must monitor the spatial relationship between the blade and everything near it, whether it's your own skin or someone else's. The tool needs a carefully monitored margin of space around it or it becomes dangerous.

The same principles apply just as well to any modern handheld tool. Imagine you're using a vacuum cleaner. Of course, the most obvious part of the task is to steer the business end of the tool to the clump of dust on the floor. But at the same time, largely beneath awareness, you're monitoring the space around the entire vacuum wand to make sure it doesn't crash into furniture or doorways and knock over vases, injure the cat, or bruise your own legs, for that matter. Even the cleaning end is treated with care. You don't just ram it into a corner. You fit it into the corner carefully, making sure not to nick the baseboard.

To give an even more universal example, most of us have learned to use a fork so well that we mistakenly think it's easy. The hard computations are hidden under the surface of consciousness. Every child has to learn the complicated task of steering the tines accurately to the piece of food you want and then to your mouth, while at the same time avoiding knocking other food off your plate, knocking over your glass of milk, or stabbing yourself in the lips. Using a fork requires an exquisite and unconscious understanding of the space around the fork.

No matter what the tool, to use it competently you must process the space around it—not just to direct the tool toward a target, but at the same time, in the background, to avoid or cushion collisions. And one simple way to solve that problem is to use the brain machinery you already have for protecting your own body parts. As I'll describe briefly in this chapter, the evidence suggests that you incorporate the tool into your body schema. It becomes a part of you, like the feathered hats I mentioned in the last chapter. You cast your margin of safety around it, encompassing it, constructing a space of potential collisions. I'm not arguing that this extension of personal space is the root of all tool use. You need a lot more skills to invent and wield a tool. But I believe a modifiable margin of safety that can be extended around a foreign object is a necessary precondition for tool use. Without that peripersonal mechanism, we might not have developed stone tool technology in the first place. We might not have progressed to our modern, complex technology. I probably wouldn't be telling you this story, because I wouldn't be able to use a keyboard or a pen to write this book, and such things would never have been invented anyway.

* * *

It had not occurred to anyone to link tool use with the peripersonal neurons until a landmark experiment by Atsushi Iriki and his colleagues in Japan, in 1996.[5,6] They trained a monkey to use a tool and studied the monkey's peripersonal neurons.

Monkeys are not known for their tools. Unlike chimpanzees, who are much closer to humans, monkeys don't typically manufacture tools in the wild. They evidently lack the cognitive ability. But they *can* learn to use tools. Cebus monkeys in South America sometimes use hammer stones to open nuts.[7,8] And you can easily train a monkey to use a novel tool. In Iriki's experiment, the monkey sat at a table, restrained in a kind of simian high chair. Treats were placed on the table and the monkey could reach out, snatch up the treats, and eat them. But sometimes a treat was placed out of reach. The monkey was given a short rake, about a foot long. With a bit of encouragement, he learned to hold the rake, reach out with it, snag the distant treat, and drag it closer until he could reach it with his hand.

After months of training, when the monkey became proficient at his task, the experimenters studied the peripersonal neurons in the parietal cortex. For example, they found a neuron that responded to the sight of any object looming into the space near the arm, within about twenty centimeters. After plotting the neuron's responses, they handed the monkey his rake. At first the tool lay passively in the monkey's hand, resting on the table. The experimenters tested the neuron's visual responses again and found no change. The neuron responded to objects in the same region of space, within about twenty centimeters of the hand. Simply holding a tool did not affect the neuron.

Then the monkey was allowed to use the tool to capture food for five minutes. After this tool-use session the tool was again left in the monkey's hand, passively resting on the table, and the experimenters once more plotted the visual responses of the neuron. Post–tool use, the neuron's responsive region had grown outward to encompass the tool. The neuron now responded to visual stimuli within about a meter, in a bubble of space that roughly overlapped the elongated tool.

The experimenters then waited fifteen or twenty minutes while the monkey sat passively, and then plotted the visual response one more time. The responsive region had shrunk again back to its original size.

About half the neurons behaved in the same way. The peripersonal neurons did not monitor a rigidly fixed region of space around the hand. Instead, that region of space could temporarily stretch, encompassing the tool.

Discovering that the peripersonal mechanism in a monkey's brain participates in tool use is all very well. It's an intriguing start. But monkeys aren't natural tool users. They don't have brain systems that evolved over millions of years for the specific purpose of managing handheld tools. Maybe after extensive laboratory training on a handheld rake, they process the tool in an idiosyncratic way that has nothing to do with human tool use. Does the peripersonal mechanism contribute to human tool use?

One of the first and most compelling lines of evidence in humans came from patients who suffered stroke damage. In the last chapter I described the neglect syndrome, a devastating disability usually caused by damage to the junction of the temporal and parietal lobes. Here I'll briefly remind you of the symptoms and then explain their relationship to tool use.

A woman suffers a stroke to her right hemisphere and wakes up in the hospital with hemispatial neglect. She responds perfectly well to items on her right side and ignores items on her left. She won't put eyeshadow on the left side of her face, dress the left side of her body, or eat the food on the left side of her plate. In her case, the neglect is limited to the space near her body. She can use a laser pointer to highlight items on a wall in front of her, whether the items are on the left or on the right. But when asked to point to items drawn on a sheet of paper in front of her, closer to her body, she points only to the right side of the page and seems unaware of the left. The brain, therefore, must have at least two spatial mechanisms, one for near space and one for far space, and in this patient the mechanism for left, near space has been damaged.[9]

Now for the truly bizarre twist to the story. Give the patient a *wooden* pointer instead of a *laser* pointer and ask her to reach out and tap on that wall to indicate items. Somehow, the neglect now extends to the wall.[10-14] She loses track of items on the left side, apparently unable to see them anymore, while still able to indicate items on the right.

A laser pointer in her hand—no problem. She can see the whole wall. A stick in her hand—spatial breakdown. She no longer sees the left side of the wall.

How can we understand this bizarre result? It seems that handing the patient a stick, like handing the monkey a rake, causes the near-space mechanism to grow outward around the tool. Given the patient's faulty near-space mechanism, the symptoms of neglect are also propagated outward along the tool.

Many studies in brain-damaged and normal healthy people have now tested how peripersonal space changes during tool use.[15-27] These experiments use many of the same techniques I described in the previous chapter, such as the extinction paradigm and the cross-cuing paradigm. Although there are some alternative interpretations,[28-30] the results point mainly to one conclusion: in the human brain, like the monkey brain, peripersonal space is stretched outward around handheld tools. For example, visual peripersonal space stretches around a wheelchair,[26] and auditory peripersonal space stretches around the cane of a blind person.[19]

To use a handheld tool, at a minimum you need three distinct sensory-motor abilities all working together. First, you need to be able to grasp the tool correctly. The brain contains a network specialized for the control of grasp.[31-33] Second, you need to aim the tool correctly toward its target. The brain also contains a network specialized for aiming the hand along a trajectory through space.[32-34] Third, as I've described throughout this chapter, you need to wrap your margin of safety around the tool. The peripersonal network may be responsible for that third ability.

These three brain networks pass extremely close to each other in the parietal lobe, as I noted in Chapter 8 (see Figure 8.1). Areas of the cortex that emphasize grasping, reaching, and peripersonal space are packed side by side. They're not perfectly insulated from each other. Instead, they overlap a little at the edges and probably have connections among each other. I think of these three parietal brain areas almost like three experts in different technical fields, all sharing an office. Sooner or later they'll start talking to each other and the combination of their expertise will produce an "ah-ha" moment. Something revolutionary will emerge. Somewhere in that nexus, that cross-fertilization of information in the parietal lobe, the spark of tool-use genius may have first appeared in the primate brain.[35-39]

Chapter 11

Why It's Sexy to Let
a Vampire Bite Your Neck,
and Other Social Consequences
of Peripersonal Space

ONE DAY I FOUND MYSELF STUCK ON A RANDOM QUESTION. It was a head scratcher. If the brain has such a powerful mechanism that monitors a margin of safety around the body and reflexively clears it of intruders, then how do we have sex?

The more I thought about that question, the more interesting the answer became.

The margin of safety is adjustable. That much is clear. It expands to buffer us from people who make us nervous and it shrinks toward friends. In monkeys it expands toward snakes and shrinks toward apples. The mechanism must have a volume knob, so to speak. With the emotional volume turned up, the shield extends farther out. The body is vigorously protected against anything looming toward it, just like in our experiment when we dripped a disinhibiting chemical on the peripersonal neurons and revved up their activity.[1] With the volume turned down, the shield weakens and shrinks back toward the skin, again as in our experiment when we dripped an inhibiting chemical on the peripersonal neurons.[1]

In the case of sex, skin-to-skin contact is necessary. And it isn't just hand-to-hand or shoulder-to-shoulder. It includes some of the most vulnerable, heavily defended parts of the body. The margin of safety must dial back to zero. The peripersonal neurons need to shut off in the moment of inspiration, or we would never be able to overcome our aversive reflexes and mate.

The more I thought about the matter, the more I realized that the shrinking of the margin of safety during foreplay and sex is more than a matter of practical geometry. It may have started out as a mechanical necessity, but it has long since turned into its own kind of evocative body language. Showing that your defensive shields are dialed back has become an act of social communication.

Just think what it means to kiss someone. Your mouth, an offensive weapon filled with teeth, presses against the other person's skin. Kissing is a way of asking, "Are you sure I can enter your defended spaces?" Letting yourself be kissed is a way of saying, "Yes, my defenses are so far down that I'm letting your biting weapon touch me."

The neck is a special participant in the mating dance. It's the part of the body most vulnerable to predators. The windpipe, the jugular vein, and the carotid artery run through it, as well as the spinal cord, so it makes a good handle for a carnivore. Powerful defensive reflexes normally protect it from intrusion by lowering the head, shrugging the shoulders, and lifting the arms to a blocking posture. It's exquisitely sensitive. If a bug lands on your neck, or a prankster creeps up behind you and touches you there, you'll typically react with a rapid defensive set. Exactly for this reason, the neck makes a good test case for sexual acceptance. Next time you kiss someone on the neck, just remember that you're putting your teeth next to your lover's jugular. Instead of cringing and scrabbling away, your lover may react with an elaborate, telegraphic opposite to the defensive repertoire. The shoulders come down rather than shrugging. The body arches back a little rather than crouching forward. The head lifts and tilts, exposing the vulnerable anatomy. This dance between the two of you tests and confirms acceptance. I'm not saying we do this intentionally. We don't intellectually think through the meaning and origin of these gestures. They're built deep into us. Humans have evolved mating signals that work because they emerged against a normal background of protective blocking and withdrawing. (The neck also plays a central role in the mating rituals of swans.)

Thumb through a fashion magazine and look at the women models. They tend to pose with their heads slightly tilted, their long necks exposed, as if at an unconscious level they're saying, "Hey, Sailor. This thingamajig that wolves go for? I'm exposing it to show how much my defenses are down for you."

I used to wonder why vampires are popularly supposed to be sexy. The connection shows up in every vampire movie or book I've encountered, right back to Bram Stoker's 1897 book *Dracula*,[2] which confused the heck out of me when I read it before puberty. Now I suspect that vampiric neck biting stirs something emotional and intuitive because it's an exaggerated version of the normal mating dance. And maybe it's not that exaggerated. People have been known to put some teeth into their kisses and leave marks.

I wonder if sadomasochism can be partly explained in the same way. I'm sure there are many varieties with many psychological causes. But maybe in some instances the masochist has an emotional longing that comes up from somewhere he can't fathom, ultimately from a human mating dance that evolved over millions of years. He has a built-in urge to communicate the fact that he's dropped his defenses, his shields are entirely down, and he's made himself vulnerable to his partner. That side to the mating ritual has gotten twisted and exaggerated in his neural circuitry. He can't satisfy that urge until he pushes it to an extreme. Likewise, maybe Christian from *Fifty Shades of Grey*[3] has an urge from the opposite end of the mating dance. He aggressively probes the defenses of his partner and confirms over and over that her shields are down.

My point here is that the margin of safety around the body can have strange, far-reaching consequences, especially in social interaction. The body's safety buffer lurks under the surface of consciousness and grows tendrils into all the rest of our culture and humanity.

A few months ago I visited China for the first time. My wife and I both gave scientific talks, which offered the excuse, and we brought along our ten-year-old son for the adventure. We took a day to visit the Great Wall. It took an exhausting climb up endless stairs just to reach the thing, with little shops along the way selling cold water, ice cream sandwiches, and trinkets. Loudspeakers hidden in the trees were blaring advertisements and admonitions in Chinese. Crowds of people were talking in an international cacophony of languages.

The wall itself, what remains of it, is a rebuild from a few hundred years ago. It's made of brick and stone and it curves and leaps along the spine of a mountain range. If you stand at a high point and look back, it gives an uncanny impression of a Chinese dragon, jointed and scaly and thin, looped and twisted over the landscape.

But I had trouble enjoying the visit. The problem, I confess, was my son. He loved the wall. He wormed through the crowd and ran up and down the long, steep slopes and curves. Every time he looked over a battlement or walked past an open window hole in one of the watchtowers, a frisson went through me. I was automatically processing the space around *his* body and the looming dangers in it. I couldn't help it.

He leaned, I cringed.

I'll bet my peripersonal neurons were firing in empathy, triggering that reflexive cringe. Maybe I'm what's called a physical empath. Or maybe it works especially powerfully between a parent and child. I saw a tourist climb up onto the narrow stony parapet and stand in a casual pose, a hundred-foot drop at her feet, while taking a selfie. And yes, I felt a twinge. My self-protective reflexes were itching. But I could at least turn away and ignore the idiot. People do die taking photos. Death by selfie—it's a medical category these days. My son, however, was never in any danger. I knew intellectually that he was safe, yet merely watching him walk up to a railing with a drop on the other side of it threw me physically off-kilter. My reaction wasn't just emotional. No, what was most striking was the *physical* muscle reaction. I couldn't help leaning back when he leaned forward.

I was relieved when we got off that wall. It was an exhausting experience.

I've noticed that the sympathetic cringe is a common component of social interaction. Sometimes you cringe in sympathy with an actual physical threat, like I did on the Great Wall. Sometimes you cringe in sympathy with an entirely abstract threat. For example, someone says, "My boss hates me. I'm pretty sure I'm getting fired in the next few days." Your reaction might be to make a grimace. You crinkle the skin around your eyes, usually one eye more than the other, raise your upper lip enough to show a bit of teeth, again more on one side, duck your head a tad, pull up a shoulder. You're expressing empathy with his employment crisis by mimicking the action you would normally make if a rock hit you in the side of the face.

Once again, the peripersonal mechanism has leaked into our social repertoire.

In the last ten years, a trickle of experiments has begun to probe the relationship between peripersonal brain areas and social behavior.[4-15] This line of experiments is still preliminary. Much remains to be done, but the results are promising. For example, if you put a person in an MRI scanner and try to activate the peripersonal network, the activity is stronger and the network stands out more clearly if you use a picture of a face looming toward the person instead of a socially irrelevant, neutral object, such as a picture of a car or a sphere.[9] If you test the size and extent of a person's peripersonal space, you'll get a different answer depending on whether the person is alone or interacting with someone else. [7,8,13] If you show me a threatening object intruding on someone *else's* peripersonal space, my *own* peripersonal network lights up.[6] These studies show that the peripersonal network in the brain has a social component. The research is so new, however, that a larger story about social processing has yet to emerge. The experiments so far barely nibble at the edges of the topic.

Personal space is essentially a second, invisible skin. And this may be why it influences so many aspects of life, including social behavior. The real skin is the most obvious interface between an animal and the rest of the world. Evolution has shaped it into an amazing diversity of scales, feathers, fur, textures, and colors. And, of course, social signals. Across the animal kingdom, the skin and its accouterments such as crests, colors, and horns form the basis of social communication. Skin may have started ancestrally as a layer of protection over the flesh, but it has come to serve dozens of outward-oriented, social and communicative purposes.

Personal space has something like the same universal impact. With personal space, the layers of protection are less obvious. They tend to go underappreciated, sliding beneath the surface of awareness. And yet they form a busy interface between us and the world. Like the physical skin, our peripersonal defenses have been shaped by evolution over millions of years and have taken on quirky add-on features. I think of those features as the feathers and horns of personal space. Some of those features have long since floated free of any specific role in defending the body. After all, the red crest of a cardinal serves none of the protective functions of skin; it's an outgrowth that sends signals to other cardinals. Just so, outgrowths of our margin of safety, our second skin, have morphed into signals that we use to communicate with each other. In the remaining chapters I'll describe how some of our most basic human gestures—smiling, laughing, and crying—may have first emerged from the defended spaces between us.

Chapter 12

The First Smile

S UPPOSE YOU AND I ARE MONKEYS. WE LIVE FIFTY MILLION years ago or more, before humans, before apes, before primates radiated all over the world, and before the evolution of many of our common facial expressions. Let's suppose (and I apologize for the indignity) that I'm a large brute of a monkey in the prime of life with impressive battle scars, while you're a younger, slimmer, bantam-weight monkey. You cringe to the side as I strut past on all fours.

The cringe is purely self-protection. It depends on ancient mechanisms in your brain. I'm a large, scary-looking visual stimulus looming into your peripersonal space. Your peripersonal neurons respond to that looming threat, monitoring my trajectory, nudging you into a protective stance. You lean away from me. Your torso hunches. Your arms pull in to protect your hands and your abdomen. Your head lowers and your shoulders lift to protect your neck, more on the side that faces me. The muscles around your eyes contract. Here the protection is nuanced. It's useful to keep your eyes open and your face turned toward me so that you can maintain a close watch. But even though your eyes are still open a slit, the surrounding muscles contract to form a protective pursing of the skin. As a consequence of this contraction of the muscles in the face, especially the muscles in the cheeks pulling the skin upward to pucker protectively around the eyes, your upper lip is pulled up, exposing a bit of your upper teeth. It isn't a snarl. It isn't a prelude to biting. The muscles involved are different from the biting, attacking, or snarling muscles that ring the mouth, and, consequently, the shape of your mouth is different. It's the shape associated with muscle contraction mainly in the cheeks that protects the eyes.

Today I merely walk past. The encounter is over in an instant.

Your reaction is a good safety policy. It puts you in a defensive crouch. But it also inadvertently broadcasts information about you—information about how you perceive me. It shows that you recognize me as so much of a potential threat that you are withdrawing. If I had the neural machinery to take advantage of that information, I could, in principle, make predictions about your behavior. I could infer that you won't attack me. I'd know that if I walk past you a second time, you're likely to give way to me again. I could peg you as non-dangerous and a hierarchical underling.

Unfortunately for me, at this early date in our speculative evolutionary history, I don't yet have the neural pathways to process that information. So let's fast-forward a few million years. We're both monkeys again. I'm still the big one, and you've just cringed away from me. But by now, evolution has shaped the brain. It's given me the tools to take advantage of the available cues. I have a set of reactions wired into me. It's not a matter of intellectual cleverness. It's not that I look at you and logically deduce the relevant information. I have something more like a cortical reflex or an instinct, like a rabbit reacting instinctively to a shadow passing overhead. When I see your stance, your body language, your raised upper lip and squinted eyes, that stimulus is an automatic trigger. It makes me feel less threatened by you and less aggressive toward you. The consequence for my own behavior is that I'm all the more likely to pass right by you. I don't challenge you. I don't preemptively attack. I don't waste the energy. And maybe I steal your food if you have any. (Again, sorry for the indignity.) I have evolved to receive the signal. The most important step in the evolution of a social signal may be the evolution of the receiver.

But we still don't really have a social signal. We have a protective cringe that you produce, and a sophisticated neural system that allows me to take advantage of your cringe to optimize my own behavior.

Let's fast-forward another few million years in our speculative timeline. We're monkeys again. Evolution has shaped the brain further, but this time giving *you* a useful, adaptive tool. Because your protective stance has a specific effect on me, triggering a predictable change in my own behavior, you have a lever by which to manipulate me. Evolution has now given you a brain system that can *mimic* that defensive stance. Even if I'm not directly looming into your personal space, even if your peripersonal neurons are not triggered and your actual defensive mechanisms are not recruited, you now have a capacity to flash a mimic defensive stance in my direction, thereby altering my behavior. It makes me less likely to attack you. And not just at that particular moment. It makes me less likely, in the future, to treat you as an aggressive adversary. It has a lingering impact on me.

Once again, this processing in the brain has nothing to do with a clever intellectual strategy. You aren't thinking to yourself, "Hmm, maybe I can fake a defensive stance, because then he'll think that I consider him to be too threatening to attack, and that will in turn cause him to ease off on his aggression. . ." No, nothing so explicit. Evolution has supplied you with a tool—a behavior that helps you negotiate the interaction with me. When in the presence of a potentially dangerous monkey with whom you don't want to fight, you reflexively flash the mimic defensive stance. You don't need to know how it works, or even *that* it works. You simply produce the action because the context triggers it in you, and the action then has a specific, useful effect.

In a similar way, a stick insect doesn't know that it's mimicking a stick or that the mimicry has the useful effect of camouflage from predators.

And just as the stick insect is a mimic and not an actual stick, your mimic defensive stance is not a real defensive reaction. It operates under a different mechanism in the brain. The peripersonal networks are probably not the same as the networks that generate the mimic defensive stance. The two behaviors are triggered under different circumstances, and they are also subtly different in their details. A true defensive stance protects you from a potentially dangerous object looming into personal space. It's exquisitely tuned to protect the most vulnerable parts of your body. In contrast, the mimic defensive stance is a way to manipulate another monkey even at a distance.

It's tuned to be easily visible. It probably involves turning your face directly toward me and exaggerating the facial components of the action. It's a separate behavior that evolved on the back of an older, defensive behavior.

What started out as one adaptation is now *three*. The original adaptation is a peripersonal mechanism that monitors the margin of safety and generates a protective stance. The second is a mechanism in the brain that perceives the protective stance in another monkey and responds to it in a stereotyped way, by reducing one's own aggression. The third adaptation is a mechanism in the brain that can generate a distorted mimic of the defensive stance and deploy it as a way of reducing aggression in others.

And now we finally have a true social signal. You produce it and I receive it (or, if you don't like being the underling monkey, I produce it and you receive it). The signal is known to scientists as the "silent bared teeth display" and has been documented in many species of monkey.[1-6] I witnessed it countless times back when I worked with macaque monkeys. They cringe down, duck the head, and raise the shoulders. The skin puckers and crinkles around the eyes, but the eyes remain open. The upper lip pulls up, and the upper teeth show. It's fundamentally a signal of nonaggression, and it's widely believed to be the origin of the human smile.

I don't like the term "silent bared teeth display." It's woefully inadequate because it focuses too much on the teeth. It misses the richness of the action, which involves the whole body. If you examine only the lifting of the upper lip, you will miss the connection to a defensive stance. Watch a low-status underling in a company, a new intern, smiling at a high-status boss, and you'll see the echo of the defensive cringe. The intern grins, teeth on display, face crinkled painfully around the eyes, body hunched, knees slightly bent, shoulders raised, hands pulled inward and curled over the abdomen or chest. At least in its more extreme manifestations a smile is still partly a servile cringe. It says, "You're the big monkey. I'm really very nonthreatening here!"

In a less extreme form, the smile is limited to the face. The other components around the body drop out. And yet it still retains the features of a mimic defensive action—the intense pursing of skin around the eyes, the upward bunching of the cheeks (an apple-cheeked smile), and the consequent lifting of the upper lip. A really strong smile mobilizes the whole face upward. A subtle smile is reduced to a tension around the eyes. Only when we fake a smile, or give a weary imitation of a smile, do we twitch our mouths and leave the eyes cold.

The nineteenth-century neurologist Guillaume-Benjamin-Amand Duchenne noticed that a genuine, friendly smile always involves the contraction of muscles around the eyes.[7] He took photos of people who tried to smile with the mouth only, avoiding the tension around the eyes. The muscles that were engaged to lift the lip were visibly different, producing a different contour to the upper lip. When he showed the photos to his colleagues, some were confused and had no idea what emotional expression was intended, and others thought the smile looked fake and cruel. The genuine smile, the one that includes the eyes, is now called a *Duchenne smile*.

Once again, to be clear, the human smile is not a defensive cringe. When you smile, you are not thereby protecting your eyes from a flying stone. You're not expressing fear. You're not anticipating an attack. But the evolutionary precursor of a smile is a defensive cringe that protects the eyes in folds of skin. A smile is an evolutionary mimic.

This evolutionary hypothesis about the origin of the smile is now widely accepted, although others may fill in the details differently. But the hypothesis was not obvious at first. Charles Darwin's original speculations miss the mark—and that is unusual. Darwin tended to be right about his evolutionary hunches. In 1872 he published a book called *The Expression of the Emotions in Man and Animals*,[8] in which he offered his own just-so stories about social signals. For example, when we're happy, we jump around a lot. All parts of the body become active as the joyful energy spreads through us and we express it to the world around us. That excess motion tends to cause excess blood flow to the face, which risks rupturing blood vessels in the eyes. To protect the eyes, the muscles around the eyes contract, holding the eyeball tight. As a consequence of that contraction, the skin of the cheeks is pulled upward and the upper lip rises. There we have a smile.

Darwin's explanation is not totally wrong. He guessed that the contraction around the eyes had something to do with defense.

He also correctly understood that the lifting of the upper lip was a mechanical consequence of the pursing of muscles around the eyes. But Darwin had a deep misunderstanding about social signaling. He focused exclusively on the sender and failed to consider the receiver. He assumed that when we feel happy, we have an intrinsic need to express that happiness. The brain releases its happy energy to the outside world. The evolutionary puzzle was to explain why a particular, quirky facial expression became the most convenient route for that self-expression. He tried his best to fill in the gaps in that line of thinking, but the line of thinking itself was mistaken.

There is no known evolutionary pressure to express oneself. There is no basic survival need for the sender to beam out signals just for the sake of expressive enthusiasm. Smiles are in the first place about manipulating the behavior of the receiver. Social signals evolve because the receiver reliably reacts in a specific way to a specific stimulus.[9-13] The sender then evolves the ability to generate and control that stimulus. It's as if the receiver had marionette strings attached, which evolved for some other, prior reason. The sender then evolves the ability to pick up and pull on those strings. Crinkling the face in a defensive set causes the receiver to be less aggressive toward you, and that is probably what drove the ability to produce a smile.

The evolutionary origin of smiling is different from its psychological origin. Most people are used to thinking about the psychological origin of smiling. I smile because I feel happy. I can't help the smile bursting out of me. It's self-expression. When that smile spreads over my face, I feel even happier because the act tickles some happy circuit in me. Sometimes I smile for the manipulative purpose of affecting someone else, like a salesman smiling at a new victim, but I try not to do that too often. That's an insincere smile, right? I try to make sure my smiles come out of me sincerely and not for some strategic reason.

But all of these psychological intuitions, as correct as they are, get in the way of understanding the evolutionary history. Evolution shaped those psychological urges in us to make us smile under useful circumstances. Ultimately, the survival advantage of a smile is the same as the survival advantage of any social signal: it manipulates the behavior of the receiver.

Chapter 13

The First Laugh

WHEN I WAS YOUNGER MY FAMILY ALWAYS HAD A DOG. When one died, we got another. For years we had a mutt named Köchel, after the musicologist who catalogued Mozart's compositions. I used to play with Köchel roughhouse style, rolling on the floor. He had a gesture he would make, opening his mouth about a half inch without showing any teeth and muttering in doggy fashion to attract my attention. It seemed to mean, depending on circumstances, either "Let's play!" or "Don't worry, I'm only playing!"

Ethologists call that gesture the open-mouth play face,[1-13] and it is common among many mammals, including primates. If I had to hazard a pretty safe guess, I'd say it evolved from opening the mouth to bite. When mammals play, they gently bite, and that open-mouth action may have morphed into a social gesture to help regulate the play and prevent injury or escalating aggression.

The great apes also have an open-mouth play face.[1,2,4,11] But they add something distinctive. When you tickle a chimp, if it's in the mood, it opens its mouth and makes a series of huffing sounds startlingly like human laughter. Gorillas and orangutans do the same thing.

Although this huffing display was noticed long ago and was even discussed by Darwin one hundred fifty years ago,[1] it has been studied systematically only more recently. For example, Dr. Marina Ross and her colleagues[11] have analyzed the sound spectrum in detail and found striking similarities between play huffing in apes and human laughter. The more genetically related a species of ape is to humans, the more similar their huffing is to human laughter. The implication is that laughter, at least the huffing part of it, evolved first in the common ancestor to apes and humans. We shared a common ancestor with chimps, gorillas, and orangutans about fifteen million years ago, so the play huffing probably has an origin before then, but after our split from other primates. We're most closely related to chimpanzees, splitting from them about five or six million years ago, and their play huffing most closely resembles ours.

And yet something happened to laughter after our split with chimpanzees. The human version of play huffing has some startling and unique characteristics. The "ha ha" is only one piece of a vastly more complex behavior. The other parts of that behavior are especially obvious in moments of intense laughter.

When somebody says the most outrageous thing that cracks everybody up, when you are helpless and overcome, rolling on the floor laughing (ROFL in today's parlance), consider what that laughter looks like. The skin wrinkles and puckers around your eyes. The muscles in your cheeks mobilize the skin upward, further padding the eyes. As your cheeks bunch upward spasmodically, your upper lip is pulled up, exposing your upper teeth. Tears are secreted. Your shoulders lift and pull forward, your torso curls forward, you hunch forward. Your arms pull in, curling around your abdomen.

In humans, laughter includes a whopping big mimic defensive reaction.

Even when the laughter is less intense, the facial defensive components are still present—the wrinkling and pursing of skin around the eyes, the upward bunching of the cheeks, and the lifting of the upper lip. Human laughter without these defensive-like components, the "ha ha" by itself, is only a hollow laugh. A sincere human laugh, like a Duchenne smile, includes a specific set of tensions, especially around the eyes. Where does the defensive-like aspect of human laughter come from?

In 2008 I suggested a possible explanation.[14] Just like the commonly accepted evolutionary explanation for the smile, this explanation for laughter depends on the reflexive actions that protect us when peripersonal space is invaded. The explanation begins with tickle-evoked laughter, which, after all, is a reaction to an intrusion into protected personal space.

Think about what happens when you tickle a child. The behavior of the child is almost like the behavior of one of the peripersonal neurons I described in earlier chapters. Those neurons act like Geiger counters for an impending collision. As your hand approaches, entering peripersonal space, the child starts to giggle and the defensive blocking and hunching begins. As your hand looms closer, the behavior becomes more intense. Finally your hand gets past the defenses and makes contact with the skin on a vulnerable part of the body. In this context of social play, the skin is so sensitive that the touch evokes a full-blown laughter, not just the huffing sound, but an entire collection of alarm shrieks, defensive blocking and retracting, a pursing of skin around the eyes, upward bunching of the cheeks, upper lip pulling up, and secretion of tears. Somehow, an exaggerated defensive set, including the release of lubricant that protects the eyes, evolved into a ritualized social signal.

To imagine how that evolution might have happened, let's turn back the clock. You and I are human ancestors, after the split with chimpanzees, which occurred around five or six million years ago. Let's say we're a couple of Australopithecines. We already have the open-mouth play face and the huffing that we inherited from our ape ancestors.

The two of us are play fighting, a fantastically useful behavior that hones basic skills. It's just as useful for primates as for tigers or wolves. But we're engaged in a special kind of play fight. We're not trying to wrestle each other or bite each other. It's a more sophisticated game. Let's say one of us is bigger and one is littler—perhaps a parent and child. (This time, to be fair, you can be the big one.) Your goal is to penetrate my defenses and make contact with a vulnerable body part. My goal is to successfully block you and protect myself. It's the simplest game of all. It's prehistoric checkers. It's endless fun.

When your hands intrude into the defended buffer of space around me, my peripersonal neurons are revved up and they trigger a coordinated defensive reaction. My body curls, my arms move into blocking postures, my shoulders lift to protect my neck, my facial muscles contract to protect my eyes. As your attacking hand looms farther into my peripersonal space, my defensive reaction becomes stronger. If you make contact with my skin, my peripersonal neu-rons fire at peak activity and my defensive reaction becomes frantic. If you hit me good, especially if you land a blow or a scratch near my eyes, my tear ducts leak lubricant to protect my eyes. None of this behavior, so far, is related to social communication. It's all basic defense of the body.

And yet that defensive behavior has an inevitable side effect. It leaks information about me to you. It's such an obvious, violent squirm that you can't possibly miss it. It advertises like a neon billboard, announcing that you've won that moment in the play fight. You've scored a hit. My defensive set broadcasts the "touché" information.

And now we have the right dynamic to evolve a social signal. Come back in a million years and the brain has evolved mechanisms to interpret that information. Here's a new version of us, a million years later. I'm giving a defensive squirm as your hand penetrates my defended spaces. You, as receiver, have pathways wired into your brain to perceive that defensive squirm, to process it in the context of the play fight, and to use it to shape your own emotions and behavior. You don't intellectually figure out what to do. It's not logical deduc-tion, and there isn't time in the fast back-and-forth of a play fight anyway. Instead, you react automatically. An instinctive system has evolved. My defensive squirm is an immediate reward to you. It says, "Touché!" It tells you that you've won the point. But it also tells you not to push the point too far. You don't want to scratch deeper or you'll injure me and jeopardize social amity. That feedback allows you to play the game without hurting me.

And yet my defensive set is still not a true social signal. I'm merely defending my body. But now that you have a predictable reaction to that defensive squirm, you've given me a potential lever to control your behavior. If I could mimic that defensive set, I could manipulate you.

Let's fast-forward another million or so years. Again, we're two play-fighting Australopithecines. By now, the brain has evolved a capacity to mimic that spasmodic defensive squirm that occurs dur-ing a play fight. By deploying that mimic defensive set I can manipu-late *your* behavior. It isn't a real defensive reaction anymore because I can produce it even when the defense is not urgent. Even if you lightly touch my skin—even if your hand comes close to my skin without touching—it triggers an exaggerated reaction from me. I'm sending out the touché signal. I'm saying, "You got me! Now give it a moment's rest and don't go too far!" The effect on you is rewarding. It tells you that you've done something clever and won a point, and it induces you to ease off for a moment before trying again.

And so we have tickle-evoked laughter, a social signal that evolved to regulate a particular kind of human interaction.

The explanation I've offered here is quite narrow. It doesn't explain where the huffing sound comes from. Why the "ha ha?" It certainly doesn't explain humor. You can't use the theory to explain why Stephen Colbert is funny and your Uncle Jim isn't. It's an open question how tickle-evoked laughter branched into the hundred other kinds of human laughter. Apparently we began to use laughter as a general social signal to manipulate each other's behavior, spreading it outside the context of a play fight.

Maybe laughter at a punch line is still a touché signal—a way for me to dispense a social reward to you, telling you in effect, "You got me. Good job. Successful punch. Now pause a little before the next joke." Maybe timing is everything in humor because it piggybacks off of a physical play fight that requires exquisite control of timing.

But what about mocking laughter, or cruel laughter, or the laughter of pure joy that has nothing to do with a joke? I'm sure I could invent many plausible explanations, as others have.[15] Human laughter is not a single thing. It's a whole category of social signals, and it must have an incredibly complex evolutionary history sprouting out of the more primitive tickle-evoked laughter.

My explanation in this book does not even try to cover that larger range. I'm not trying to explain laughter so much as trying to show how a fundamental, protective personal space has shaped us in unexpected ways. My proposal focuses on why human laughter resembles defensive behavior. Human laughter may have evolved originally from play fighting in which one player penetrates the defended spaces of the other player. It now retains many characteristics of the defensive reaction.

Chapter 14

The First Cry

I ONCE SAW A GROWN MAN CRYING IN PUBLIC. HE WAS sitting on a park bench with a friend sitting next to him. The sight was shocking and disturbing to me. The man was curled forward, his arms pulled over his chest as if guarding himself, his shoulders hunched and shaking. The expression on his face stood out like a mask. I could see his upper teeth. His lips were pulled back hard and the flesh around his eyes was crinkled and puckered. Tears were coming out. He was shuddering. I didn't know what he was crying about, but it must have been a devastating tragedy. He seemed unable to catch his breath. He took a large, noisy inhalation, his head lifting slightly. When he expelled the breath, the sound that came out was just a little peculiar. Suddenly it didn't quite sound like normal grief. It started as a strangled noise and then blasted out in loud bursts until I realized: the dude wasn't crying. He was laughing. He was laughing so hard I thought he might fall off the bench and die. And then the scene made a lot more sense. People, especially men, laugh in public more often than they cry.

The similarity between extreme laughter and crying is startling. Sometimes only context can separate them. They both share traits with the smile. I suggest that this similarity is not an accident. It is not dictated by the limited degrees of freedom of facial muscles. We humans have many other facial expressions that don't use the same muscles in the same ways, such as an angry face, ashamed face, or disgusted face.[1] Three expressive gestures in particular, smiles, laughter, and crying, share point-for-point many of the features of a defensive set. My proposal is that all three social signals ultimately evolved, along different paths and in different ways, from the reflexive actions that protect the body from impending impact. They all crawled out from our personal space.

Crying is a difficult behavior to study from an evolutionary perspective because only humans do it. Other animals make distress cries. We call it crying when a puppy whimpers. But it isn't the same as human crying. Even newborn human babies don't properly cry. They wail without tears. Within a few months, true crying develops.

Most attempts to explain the origin of crying focus on the tears. Tear production does seem to be the lowest-threshold part of the behavior. Sad thought, moist eyes. But the tears are only one out of a large set of components. Human crying includes a secretion of tears, a contraction of facial muscles—I could repeat the whole list again—a pursing of skin around the eyes, a bunching upward of the cheeks, a lifting of the upper lip, a lowering of the head, a raising of the shoulders, a hunching of the torso, a pulling of the arms into a blocking posture around the abdomen or chest or face, and a repeated aspiration that is sometimes voiced. Many of these components match a normal defensive set.

Other animals solicit comfort by making noise. No other animal solicits comfort by making noise while leaking lubricant out of the eyes and partially mimicking the actions that normally protect the face from an impending collision. Why do humans cry like this?

I might as well start with Darwin. He began the whole just-so evolutionary game about social signals with his 1872 book, *The Expression of the Emotions in Man and Animals*.[2] His explanation of crying begins with babies screaming when in distress. In his speculation, the extreme forcing of air through the windpipe excites blood flow to the face. That extra blood flow risks rupturing the blood vessels in the eyes. (Here his explanation overlaps with his account of the smile.) To protect the eyes, the facial muscles contract, packing the eyeballs in a tight, protective cushion. The squeezing of muscles around the eyes, along with the air pressure from the screaming, forces fluid out of the tear ducts. In the first few months of life, this process is not fully functional, but soon the full crying behavior is established.

Another account of crying was proposed in 1963 by the zoologist R. J. Andrew.[3] He argued that crying mimics a case of contaminants in the eyes. It evolved as a way to express distress.

Many other theories have been proposed, but I won't bother to describe them here. Previous accounts such as Darwin's and Andrew's were misguided because they focused on the sender of the signal. They focused on why a person would cry when sad or distressed. But crying, like any other social signal, is not fundamentally about self-expression. It's about manipulating a receiver. Crying solicits comfort. When I see someone crying, I have an instinctive, wired-in urge to provide comfort. At the very least, I try to do no harm. It's hard for me to stay angry or feel aggressive toward a person who is crying. The behavior is almost like a shield put up by the crier that acts by blunting harm from other people. To understand where crying comes from, we must start with its impact on the receiver.

Although other animals don't cry in the human sense, they do provide comfort to each other. Of course adults comfort infants. But I was struck by certain circumstances in which adults comfort adults. Let's say we're both chimps and we belong to the same family group. One day you beat the crap out of me over food. You might even hurt me quite badly. After the fight, you'll comfort me. Other chimps from the same group might also comfort me by grooming or touching me. In bonobos, the comforting sometimes takes the form of makeup sex. Underlying these instances of adult-on-adult comforting is a burst of aggression that threatens social amity. The social amity is crucial in a highly cooperative species. Because fights are inevitable, it's adaptive to have a mechanism for comforting the fight victim afterward.

Given all of that, here is my proposed evolutionary account of crying.

Sometime after our ancestors split from the chimp lineage, when we were Australopithecines three or four million years ago, we lived in cooperative social groups. But we were an ornery bunch prone to fighting. Our fights were not pleasant. A wonderful analysis of the bone structure of Australopithecines, by the anthropologists David Carrier and Michael Morgan,[4,5] suggests how our ancestors might have fought each other. In those scientists' interpretation, the facial bones are buttressed to withstand the stress of a blow, much like the facial bones of a bighorn sheep are buttressed to withstand the stress of a head collision. Moreover, according to the same authors, the bones of the hand are shaped to optimize curling the fingers into a fist and delivering a forceful punch. The implication is that Australopithecines engaged in ritual fighting by making fists and punching each other in the face.

Many species have unique, sometimes elaborate methods of fighting. I mentioned the head-crashing of bighorn sheep. Deer fight with antlers. Giraffes swing and bang their necks together. Hippos fight with wide-open mouths. Humans ball their hands into fists and punch each other in the face. That mode of fighting, as far as I know, is unique to us.

Suppose you and I are Australopithecines in a fight and you win. You punch me hard in the nose. You've penetrated my peripersonal space and made violent contact with my face. All my usual defensive reflexes spill out. The skin purses around my eyes, my upper lip pulls up, my eyes water from the trauma to my nose, my head ducks down, my shoulders rise, my arms pull across my torso or into a blocking posture across my face.

It's no advantage to you to make an enemy of me, or to make me so afraid that we can't cooperate in the future. You need a mechanism for recognizing when you've won, especially when you've gone too far and hurt me. That mechanism should trigger you to reduce your aggression and offer comfort. In that way, you can repair the social amity after the fight. It's a much-needed mechanism for a socially cooperative but fight-prone species.

But how do you judge when you've gone far enough and it's time to comfort me? My extreme defensive reaction offers the most obvious signal. In this hypothesis, the hominid brain evolved to receive that particular signal. When you see me act out an extreme defensive set, the kind normally triggered by a violent punch to the nose, it triggers an instinctive reaction in you. You reduce aggression and give comfort. The adaptation is a simple, effective way to help preserve social amity after a fight.

Now we reach the Machiavellian part of the story. I can take advantage of your wiring. If I mimic that particular type of defensive reaction, I should be able to press your buttons and extract comfort from you. In effect, I'm hacking the system. Maybe we never got into a fight. Maybe you have no aggression toward me. Maybe nobody has hurt me. My peripersonal neurons are not involved and I'm not making an actual defensive movement. It doesn't matter. If I sidle up to you and display that particular kind of behavior, it will push the right buttons to extract comfort from you.

Of course, I don't figure that out intellectually. I'm not a strategic genius of an Australopithecus. I have no idea why I produce that behavior. Evolution has built it into my brain. All I know is, when I need comfort, that behavior comes out of me instinctively, and it works pretty well—it usually evokes comfort from you, if I don't do it too often.

In this hypothesis, crying is not a facial protective action. It's a mimic. The mimic roughly resembles, but is not exactly the same as, the original. Watch a tennis player get whacked in the face by a ball and the reaction is brief, efficient, and not nearly as dramatic as a crying jag. In contrast, the mimic behavior is exaggerated and extended. It can be stretched out for minutes at a time. And it's noisy, because the noise helps attract attention. The mimic behavior is tuned not to protect the body, but to evoke a reaction in the receiver. Crying is a distortion and exaggeration of a defensive set.

It's also what one might call a third-order adaptation. The evolution of crying in this account, just like the evolution of smiling and laughing, involves three adaptations, each layered on top of the next. The first layer is a defensive mechanism that monitors peripersonal space and protects the body. The second layer, piggybacked on the first, is an instinctive reaction to the defensive behavior—providing comfort after a fight. The third layer, piggybacked on the second, is an exaggerated mimic of the defensive set that comes out as crying, and that triggers comforting behavior in others.

I find something sublimely ridiculous about Australopithecines punching each other in the nose, thereby giving us one of the most poignant of human emotional expressions. But this may be how social signals normally evolve—through an elaborate, crazy, zigzag dance between sender and receiver.

Chapter 15

The Personal Dimension
of Personal Space

I THOUGHT I'D SHARE A DIFFICULT EXPERIENCE MY FAMILY had a few years ago. It illustrates almost every important point I want to make about personal space. When the ability to process personal space is compromised, almost everything is affected—sometimes in weird, unexpected, even devastating ways. It's not just a matter of academic science, of monitoring neurons and measuring reaction times. Personal space is a real thing that impacts real lives culturally, socially, and emotionally. This story is difficult for me because it involves my son. But I think it's important to tell because—as I discovered—ignorance is the enemy. People should know.

I'll try not to get too high up on my soapbox about the condition called *dyspraxia*. It's sometimes called the hidden disability because so few people know about it and so few people—teachers, parents, or children—can see it even when it's standing right in front of them crashing into things.

Dyspraxia is a gap between what you know in your head and what you can do in the physical world. It's a difficulty with movement control, especially when learning new, complex skills.[1]

Every case of dyspraxia is unique, and therefore it's probably not valid to take one case as emblematic of the whole. For my son, one of the main components of his particular form of dyspraxia was a failure of normal personal space. That may partly explain why his disability was so hard for people to spot—for myself, his teachers, and the experts. After all, the mechanisms of personal space run mostly outside of consciousness. We monitor the space around us and judge the personal space of other people without even knowing we're doing it. As a result of this under-the-surface processing, when most people look at a child who has trouble with personal space, they find it hard to pin down what's wrong. They get an uncomfortable vibe without knowing why. For my son, it was that hidden quality of dyspraxia that harmed him most as his teachers began to turn on him and ultimately kicked him out of his school.

By the time my son was four, we realized that something was wrong. He was happy, smart, talkative, and clumsy. That clumsiness seemed to grow more and more obvious. He could trip over a flat floor. We watched him once fall on his face without the slightest sign of putting up his hands to protect himself. He could spontaneously fall out of a chair. He crashed into furniture and people. He had a penchant for leaning against random people in line at the supermarket. His legs were always blotched with bruises as if he were a young giraffe with his spots just coming out. He had no trouble with his vision and knew the obstacles were there, but he couldn't seem to organize his avoidance responses. His protective buffer zone was disorganized.

He spilled his milk more often than not. Most of us have an unconscious tendency to steer our hands and arms away from a milk glass as we reach for something else. It's one of the functions of peripersonal space. He lacked that ability so completely, it sometimes seemed like his elbow had a magnetic attraction to the glass. Sitting across the table from him, I was more aware of that glass in his space than he was.

Peripersonal space normally operates in the background. It keeps track of objects in your margin of safety without any need for focused attention. As a result, you automatically accommodate to the clutter of objects around you. But my son spectacularly lacked that automatic process. If he paid focal attention to an object, he could reach for it or grasp it. As soon as he stopped attending to the object, it disappeared from his world. Sooner or later he'd crash into it and then look startled, as though surprised it was still there.

He did not totally lack a protective shell. We noticed that he was hypersensitive to touch. It was as if his warning system had been concentrated onto the skin and had little or no extension into the space around him.

As time passed, we noticed more difficulties. When he held basic, everyday implements in his hands, he didn't seem to know how to use them. He could hold a pencil but could barely write. He couldn't use a fork. If he tried, he was likely to knock the rest of his food off the edge of the plate. None of these tools seemed to become natural extensions of his hands.

We saw these hints for years, but children develop at different rates and we kept our alarm at bay until first grade. Then the problems in school began.

For a kid with a sunny disposition and an electric fascination for new information, whether about crocodilians or any other topic, he surprised us by his growing dislike of school. He said that he felt like the dummy of the classroom. And that ability to articulate his worries was typical of him, too. He had an amazing conceptual precision to his thinking and his language. He was smart and friendly but felt like an outsider at school, increasingly embarrassed by the comparison between himself and the other children. If anything, his social sensitivity made the situation worse. He didn't have the luxury of blissful ignorance. He couldn't help but notice that he was different and was treated differently. For one thing, his writing was unlike anyone else's. It was a strange, undecipherable scribble, while everyone else was getting along pretty well. He didn't even walk through a room or sit in a chair quite like anyone else. Maybe because of those subtle differences, he was bullied by some of the other kids. And he felt that the teachers blamed him. They told him constantly that he just wasn't trying hard enough—and that comment, he explained, was the most frustrating part because *he* knew how hard he was trying.

We didn't understand the depth of the problem. Of course, we still don't fully. Dyspraxia is subtle and poorly studied, even though it affects an estimated one in fifteen or twenty children[1]—perhaps one in every classroom. The explanations I can give now came gradually, frustratingly, over many years, and like so many case studies in dyspraxia, they may apply extremely well to one child and imperfectly to others. I find it ironic that I studied the brain basis of personal space for decades and yet had so much trouble recognizing it up close in real life. That's the hidden disability for you. I thought my son had issues controlling his fingers during writing. Fine-motor coordination was the catch phrase. That was true, as far as it went. And yet that pat explanation left us with a series of contradictions.

For example, on close examination there seemed to be nothing wrong with his fingers or his eyesight. He was pretty good at Legos. His grip strength was solid. So why did he have such trouble writing? And given that his writing was undecipherable—everything piled on top of everything else in a deranged way—how come he sometimes managed to write a few words perfectly?

We now know that he couldn't build a good spatial foundation from the core of his body. Personal space, after all, is an outward extension of the body schema. Without that anchor point in his body, he couldn't build up a proper understanding of the space around him or coordinate movements and postures of his arms and hands within that space. He lacked the foundation on which the more delicate writing movements are normally built. He couldn't properly wrap his peripersonal space around a pencil in his hand. And he couldn't judge the spacing on a page. For example, other children start writing at the top left margin. My son may have learned the concept, but in practice he would plop the first mark down anywhere, sometimes in the center, sometimes on the right side of the page. He tended to neglect the left side of the page, a common spatial disturbance in dyspraxia sometimes called pseudo-neglect.[2] True clinical neglect is when specific damage to the brain, such as a stroke, erases a person's ability to orient to one side of space. It's stark. But children can develop a more subtle pseudo-neglect if they can't fully tune up their mechanisms for processing space.[2]

In any complicated motor act, like juggling, when you first learn it you have to think through every movement you make. Nothing is automatized. Sometimes you hit a groove and you can manage the trick for a moment, but it requires ferocious concentration and a little luck. Then just as suddenly, it falls apart and the balls come crashing down. You may understand the concept of juggling and you may be able to describe verbally exactly what you need to do, but you can't do it consistently until you learn it to the point of automaticity, when the movements and postures roll by underneath consciousness. It's exactly that learning to the point of automaticity that's so hard in dyspraxia.

Just so with my son and his writing. Every now and then, on a good day, he could manage to write a word or two perfectly with immense concentration before the skill fell apart. He certainly understood writing at a conceptual level. Making it come out was the problem. Writing required full-on mental effort for every posture and movement. He could not learn to automatize it. That meant he had occasional good moments but mostly an illegible scrawl. And that inconsistency was the source of much misunderstanding. To teachers, it meant that he *could* do it and therefore on most days he must be lazy or defiant. And this blame game, it turns out, is one of the most common problems in dyspraxia.[1] Teachers and parents think they see an uncooperative child. My son's bad writing became his own fault and was punishable by revoking recess. He'd stay in the classroom alone with the teacher, laboring unsuccessfully over practice sentences. He was bitter about the punishment because he wanted to play woodchip tag with his friends. (We never did learn what woodchip tag was.)

Math was equally difficult. One doesn't think of math as a matter of personal space, but consider how it's learned. Kids are taught to point and count. If your spatial skills are so lousy that you can't point accurately to a series of small items on the page, then you can't get a leg up on first-grade math. Compounding the problem, if you can't write the numbers, if 2 + 2 = 4 ends up as an inky black hole and the next problem gets written down on top of the last one, then embarrassment and stress will turn you away from the subject all together. Children with dyspraxia tend to have something called *dyscalculia*—a difficulty in basic math. The reason is not well understood, but in the case of my son a poor handle on space seems to have been a contributor. He could do arithmetic in his head when he was relaxed, and as a first-grader he even had a grasp of sophisticated concepts such as negative numbers and fractions. But if you put a pencil in his hand and forced him to negotiate the space on a sheet of paper, he instantly lost all math capacity. His mind was so occupied with the immense task of coordinating the pencil that he had no mental space left for the math.

As to reading, if you can't hold the book steady and coordinate your head and eyes, if your spatial sense isn't refined enough to resolve the positions of individual letters, then reading becomes nearly impossible. Eventually he discovered his own trick. He would crouch on the rug in front of a big padded chair in our living room, prop his book up in the chair where it remained perfectly still, rest his chin on his cupped hands on the edge of the seat to stabilize himself, and read quite well. Maybe by taking the book out of his hands and placing it more distant from his body he had removed it from peripersonal space. Sometimes children find their own way.

I noted in an earlier chapter that neuroscience distinguishes between at least two different ways that the brain processes space. One set of brain areas processes the space with respect to the body—*egocentric space*. Separate networks in the brain process space with respect to external landmarks, such as the shape of a room, the plan of a building, or the layout of a city—environmental space, or *allocentric space*. My son's problems lay with egocentric space, not allocentric space. In fact he was so good at allocentric space that for a long time we didn't realize he had any difficulty with spatial processing at all. He was like the neglect patients who can bisect a line at a distance with a laser pointer, but can't do it on a piece of paper right in front of them.[3]

When he was six, he and I were standing in the backyard looking up at the roof of our house. I was pointing to a tin ventilation pipe jutting up from the slates. "That's where the mouse must have got in," I said. We had recently found a dead mouse in the dryer duct. A horrible and smelly misadventure.

My son gently took hold of my hand as he looked up at that pipe on the roof. It's in his personality to be diplomatic. He said, "It could be. You might be right. But then the pipe would have to go a long way sideways. Because that's not where the dryer is. It's more over there." And he pointed directly into the brick wall toward where the dryer was.

I had to do some mental gymnastics, imagining myself walking through the house around this bend and through that doorway, to see if he was right. And he was. Not that he's a genius, and not that I'm a *total* idiot. My point is that he had no difficulty with certain kinds of geometric reasoning, even very complex reasoning. But personal space, such as pointing to items right up close on the page in front of him? That was hard. No other example I can think of better illustrates how his difficulty was more with space itself than with muscle control. The physical act of pointing was no problem. Whether he was pointing in allocentric space or egocentric space made all the difference.

And yet all these difficulties with personal space that I've described so far, as handicapping as they were in school and at home, were small beans compared to the social impact. Personal space plays its most profound human role in the social domain. That invisible bubble of protected space, the space in which you don't want other people, creates the scaffold for all other social transactions. It places us in a great social honeycomb of decorous relationships. We don't usually notice it because it operates smoothly in the background. We unconsciously construct our own buffer zone and evaluate how other people are creating their buffer zones, and then we hang all our social niceties and judgments on that scaffold. Only when that construction goes wrong does it obtrude into consciousness. And then people are—for lack of a better term—weirded out. Social generosity comes crashing down. And that's what happened to my son at school.

The disaster unfolded gradually. The worst part started after Christmas vacation in first grade. Under the stress of his difficulties, he began to rock in school. He would sit in his chair in increasing social isolation and rock repetitively. His movements were never quite normal in any context and the rocking was no exception. Apparently it looked more like jiggling tofu. At any rate, it disturbed the teachers, who believed—I am not making this up—that it was a sexual gesture. A six-year-old was engaging in sex acts and disrupting the class. Nothing they said could make him stop. He would just look at them as if he didn't know what they were talking about. And he probably didn't. Stress stereotypies like rocking are deep, automatic, unconscious actions. Often the child is far away, withdrawn into his own world and blocking out the unwelcome reality as hard as possible. My son certainly had no idea of the interpretation put on him by the teachers and classroom aids, although he caught the general drift that they found him disgusting. They told him he should go to the bathroom to do that, and he had not the foggiest idea what they were talking about. Go to the bathroom to sit at his desk?

He told us once that the teachers had yelled at him for touching the rug during story time. He ended up in the principal's office for that one. He was almost in tears with frustration because, as he put it, how can you *not* touch the rug when you're *sitting* on it? This little boy was totally mystified about his teachers' complaints.

The teachers insisted we give our son a talking-to. Since he was defying the teachers, maybe he'd listen to his parents. Well, we tried, and it didn't work. We didn't even know precisely what the behavior was, since he didn't do it at home. He was stressed at school, not at home. From the point of view of the school, I guess we looked like remiss parents. In reality, our concern had gone off the charts. We sent him to a child therapist who confirmed our general guess. He suffered from acute performance anxiety in school brought on by his dyspraxia, especially his inability to write, and it was causing the stress rocking.

We also sent him to a private occupational therapist who tried to build up his finger strength by having him knead Play-Doh. That intervention was meant well but shows how little any of us understood his dyspraxia at that time. His difficulty ran much deeper than finger strength. It had to do with the strength and posture of his body core and the construction of space that builds off of that core. It had to do with the thousand competencies that depend on peripersonal space. We had no concept of the spatial problems he was struggling against, but we were sure that he wasn't lazy, defiant, or a six-year-old sex deviant. He was a little boy trying his best against a mysterious and invisible disability.

What happened next may seem like it has nothing to do with personal space, but of course it does. My point is exactly this: when personal space malfunctions, everything else suffers. The ripple effect hits every aspect of life. Nothing shows this pattern more starkly than the social interaction between a child and the rest of the world. A small dysregulation early in life can lead to a general systems collapse.

The principal of the school, convinced of the sex-act interpretation, reported us to child protective services on the theory that we might be abusing him. Now we were in the gears of a system. I understand the philosophy that it's better for a principal to play it safe. If there's a doubt, make the call and alert the authorities. But there's a flip side to reporting a family to social services. It puts an incalculable stress on the family that nobody can fathom who hasn't personally experienced it. There is a panic at the back of a parent's mind. Can this turn into a runaway nightmare? Can they take our child away? Meanwhile, children are like sensitive seismographs for detecting stress in the family, no matter how hard the parents try to hide it. Stress the family, and you stress the child. And in the case of my son, that made everything worse. The rocking, the withdrawal at school, the inability to concentrate calmly on the topics he needed to learn, it was all exacerbated.

A man came to the house and interviewed us, one at a time. He was very nice and seemed a little angry at the behavior of the school. He kept asking us, why didn't they try a different classroom? That's the first thing you do when a child is stressed. You put him in a different classroom. Why didn't they bring in the school psychologist? Why didn't he have special support to help with his handwriting?

We tried to get the school to offer support for his handwriting, but we hit a snag. To get the help, the district told us, we first needed an evaluation. The people who would evaluate him were the same people who thought he was engaging in disruptive sex acts. They told us that if they evaluated him, they were likely to put him in the "emotionally disturbed" category. A label like that sounded like bad news to us. It didn't sound like a gateway to better movement therapy. It sounded more like a prelude to kicking him out of school and sending him to a special institution. It could potentially derail the rest of his life.

The conflict with the school grew out of two irreconcilable views of the same little boy. In one view, he had difficulty organizing his movements and a rapidly escalating anxiety, almost a panic, as he saw how different he was from everyone else. Nobody at the school was helping him with his disability, and the social stigma was spiraling out of control. In the other view, a much less forgiving view, a scary child had no real movement issues and no excuses, but was uncooperative, sexualized, and emotionally threatening to others. No attempt to tell him off seemed to penetrate his defiant attitude. The two perspectives were unbridgeable. We had our son assessed by expert after expert, and each one diagnosed the same consistent pattern of spatial and movement difficulties compounded by anxiety. The people at school thought they saw something so obvious that it didn't require them to consult an expert of their own.

In retrospect, I understand better why the school had such a perception problem. In the simplest definition, personal space is the virtual padding we maintain between each other. My son had no good mechanism to judge or maintain it. When he stood on line, he leaned against the kids in front or behind him. The teachers described a strange barging-through behavior where he'd push his way between other people on his path across the classroom. When the class sat on the floor for story time his body would splay everywhere, his feet kicking one kid, his hands flopped into another child's lap. When he played games, such as the ever-popular zombie game—well, zombies may be the only game where a poor sense of personal space is appropriate, and yet he probably misjudged that as well. Not only was he touching and bumping all day long, but he was often engaging in that disorganized wiggle that disturbed the teachers. And he did it all with a friendly smile as if he thought he was a regular kid, which seemed to frustrate the teachers more than anything else. No matter how many times he was told, he wouldn't correct his behavior—for the good reason, as we now know, that it wasn't intentional behavior. He simply couldn't correctly process the space around his body or finesse his movements in that space. Might as well tell a paraplegic to stop being disrespectful in his wheelchair and get up like a normal person.

The principal, apparently losing all patience with this incorrigible child, finally kicked him out. The school asserted (in writing, no less) that he was "sexually assaultive" and expelled him. They carefully didn't call it an expulsion, but it turns out that legally, that's what it was.

They cited a series of incidences in which he had bumped and leaned against other children and one instance in which, as we found out later, he actually *was* playing zombies with a group of kids. The crowding and bumping looked disturbing, grotesque, even frightening, and finally the principal had found a way to label it and get rid of him.

It's a long, frightening drop from a poor sense of personal space to being kicked out of school as a sex assaulter.

Our son was out of school for nearly two months. It was the most surreal time of my life and maybe will turn out to be for his, too. I'm sure he'll never forget it. Every day he'd ask when he could go back. As much as school stressed him, it was also his world. He had tried hard to do well, he had wanted to fit in, and he had failed. He thought he had broken a rule and been kicked out by angry teachers. It's telling that he had no idea of the real reason. He understood the mechanics of personal space so poorly that he still had no concept of what had gone wrong. He thought that the class bully had maliciously told lies about him and turned his teachers against him. We explained that his teachers, who were trying to be helpful, merely thought he needed a break—but I'm not sure he ever really believed that explanation. A few times, on the weekends, he wanted to take a walk to the school and visit his friend the big wooden bear sculpture next to the front door.

And yet I was relieved that he was finally out of that school. I was sure we'd find a better way forward.

We retained a lawyer. I won't go into the complexities of that legal battle, but it was a long, intricate process. My wife and I became rather better versed in New Jersey education law than we had ever expected to be. In brief, we wanted our son back in school as soon as possible, but not *that* school. We visited several options in the area, my son coming with us, observing and offering his thoughtful opinion. One school had a dog, which he liked. Another had turtles in the court-yard, a definite plus. Private schools had their advantages, but public schools had better services for special needs, if you could get them.

The best option was a public school in the same district. We knew the school well and personally knew the principal. The place was known for its welcoming attitude and exceptional support for special-needs children. Since our son probably needed a classroom aide to help with his writing and occupational therapy to help with his movement control, the school seemed the ideal choice. But the district denied our request.

It's hard to breathe at your own court hearing. Everyone is quiet and on good behavior. The tension is sickening. The judge, an older woman with iron-gray hair, sat at a great raised wooden bench and looked down at us. The bench was out of proportion to the rest of the room, which was tiny and crooked like an architectural accident. Only the lawyers were allowed to speak. I remember the principal of the old school waving at us from the other side of the room and smiling a big fake smile, as if we were old friends. She must have had no psychological comprehension.

The lawyer for the district made the case that our son was sex-ually assaultive. Everything had been tried to stop his threatening behavior, and nothing had worked. He was defiant. He was a danger to staff and children and therefore had to be removed from the pub-lic school. The district had stuck to its own assessment, apparently without consulting anything like an expert on child behavior or child psychology. I remember the judge leaning forward across her bench, looking over her glasses at the district lawyer, not in anger, but in pure astonishment, and saying, "This is a six-year-old boy, right? We're talking about a six-year-old boy?"

On our side we presented letters from a child psychiatrist, a child therapist, and a pediatrician, all of whom had met our son and formed their own professional opinions. The experts suggested that the school had constructed a drastic, harmful misinterpretation of a little boy with a movement disability. As the psychiatrist laconically put it, "He told me he had embraced a classmate in the lunch room while playing zombies. I never regarded this conduct as sexually predatory as apparently school staff do."

The judge ruled in our favor. By court order our son was enrolled in the school we requested, with a classroom aide and what is called a 504 plan to address his disability.

When you're stuck in the gears of a system, you never know how far its momentum will go. A school administration, like any bureaucracy, is slow to admit a mistake, no matter how absurd the mistake may be, or change direction, no matter how damaging the trajectory. But finally someone in a position of authority had the common sense to help us.

Sometimes I wonder what went through the minds of the new school staff on that day my son showed up for class, almost eight months into first grade. Did they expect a monster child based on the intel from the previous school? Someone pugnacious, angry, sexualized and threatening?

They assigned him to their most experienced first-grade teacher, who agreed to accept the extraordinary challenge. They placed their most accomplished classroom aide in a seat beside him. The school's child psychologist, one of the most lauded in the area, oversaw the operation. They were taking no chances with the dangerous wild-child. In walked a little boy, bushy-headed and with a shy smile. Very quiet, preternaturally observant. Friendly to everybody, both kids and adults. Easy-going in a conversation. Diplomatic. Sharing. Gentle. Never egotistical. Never aggressive, never angry. Sometimes nervous, inclined to sit funny and rock in his chair. And, to the trained eyes on him at the new school, whoppingly obviously suffering from a major difficulty organizing his movements in the space around his body. He really did tend to fall out of his chair. And to crowd people without understanding the normal spacing between bodies. And he could not organize letters spatially on the page. The teacher discovered that he had a good math mind as long as you engaged him verbally. If you asked him to do anything on paper, he would freeze up in anxiety.

And he was exceptionally empathetic. One day, the school went on a field trip. As the class assembled outside to wait for the bus, a disabled student with leg braces joined the group. The other kids were shy and avoided the boy with the braces, but as he tried to climb up the steps of the bus, my son seemed magnetically attracted to him and came over to help. They sat next to each other the whole trip, chatting. According to the assistants who chaperoned, that little boy with the braces was the happiest kid on the bus. One of the popular kids had befriended him. I think people who know what it's like to have a handicap develop a special empathy. They've experienced bullying and exclusion and they can't bear to see it happen to another person. I like to think that's the lesson my son learned from the mistreatment of the old school.

The psychological healing was a harder journey than you might imagine. In a way, my son was in mourning. Difficult as that old school may have been, he had grown accustomed to it. He was burdened with a sense of failure and a child version of posttraumatic stress disorder. The experts warned us that it might take several years for him to come to terms with that past. Bullying has a long-lasting impact, and the psychological bruises go even deeper when the bullies are adults.[4]

For a long time, even when he seemed adjusted to the new school and on good terms with everybody, he had a skittishness, a dreadful worry that he might break a rule. Here's one example. In second grade he tripped and broke his leg on the playground. Well, breaking a leg is probably common among dyspraxic children. It was a hairline fracture and he was able to hobble back to the classroom. But he wouldn't tell anyone. Somehow he didn't trust the teachers enough. They wondered why he wasn't doing his work. He sat at his desk, disengaged, inattentive, sweating, and for two hours they couldn't figure out the problem. Finally he admitted that something was wrong with his leg.

Even two years later he would drop occasional, poignant comments about his old school. My wife was watching a Hulk movie with him, one of the old ones with Lou Ferrigno as the green mon-ster. After the movie, which he liked very much, he said, "I wish the Hulk would go to my old school, in the night sometime when nobody's there to get hurt"—yes, he actually did add that proviso—"and smash it up. Then they'd have to close the school and no other kids would get treated like I was."

Every day, the psychological poison was dripping out of him. He was regaining confidence in school. But we still faced the problem of his movement control. The underlying handicap was unresolved despite enormous effort. He had a classroom aide, he had social skills training for personal space, he had occupational therapy and physical therapy both in school and privately. But his movement progress was shockingly slow. We simply did not understand his dyspraxia. It took us years to understand the deep confusion of space, and until that confusion was addressed, nothing seemed to stick.

It was an astute professional who pointed out his trouble with bal-ance. There's a simple procedure, called the Romberg test.[5] Stand on one foot, close your eyes, and see how many seconds you can maintain your balance. Well, let's call it the basic Romberg if you stand square on two feet and close your eyes. Even at that, he couldn't manage more than a few seconds. He had a devastatingly poor vestibular sense. It was hard to spot because he had partly learned to compensate with vision. Take away the vision, and he lost all sense of where he was.

That vestibular discovery was a light-bulb moment. The inner ear contains the vestibular apparatus, a set of semicircular tubes and chambers filled with fluid. Every turn or dip of the head causes the fluid to counter-rotate, which in turn is registered by microscopic, sensitive hair cells lining the walls of the apparatus. To say that the inner ear is necessary for balance is a drastic simplification. It tracks acceleration and rotation of the head in all directions while monitor-ing the arrow of gravity. It keeps track of your spatial relationship to the world immediately around you and is one of the most important building blocks of the physical sense of self and of egocentric space.[6,7] The peripersonal neurons that I described throughout this book are powerfully affected by vestibular signals.[8,9] That peripersonal net-work monitors the space near the body through touch, vision, and hearing, with the vestibular sense as a glue that helps to bind the signals together. Without it, those neurons might not be able to build their properties correctly. You wouldn't know where you are with respect to the world or where objects are with respect to you. The peripersonal mechanism would be crippled.

Most of us have some notion of what it feels like to temporarily lose vestibular regulation. Just drink a little too much. The alcohol gets into your blood, is filtered into your vestibular system, and lowers the density of the tissues by a tiny amount[10]—just enough to make the sensory receptors react abnormally. The signals coming from your vestibular apparatus become confused, inconsistent, mismatching the evidence of your eyes, and the brain has trouble interpreting.

Maybe that's what personal space was like to my son—a dizzy blur of items spinning around unaccountably. It's hard to maintain the right spacing with other people when you can't get a fix on where they are. You lean and bump. No matter how many times the teacher tells you to respect someone else's personal space, it does no good. You respect it! You really do! You just can't *see* it very well. It's hard to walk through a room without crashing into something or someone. You need a fierce, focused attention, your eyes fixed on the ground—like a drunk person trying to pass a sobriety test. And because your eyes are fixed on the ground all the time, people think you're ignoring them. It's hard to sit upright in a chair. You're prone to fall out of it. You don't know quite where your arms are in the space around you, where your hands are, or, for that matter, where the piece of paper is or the ruled lines on it. Good luck learning to write. Or point and count. Or use a knife and fork. If you can't even wrap your personal space around your body correctly, how can you extend it around a handheld tool? In your mind you may understand the world. You may have a perfect conceptual grasp of space and time, a map of the important items in your life. But that ever-changing space immediately around you? That's chaos.

I don't want to claim that a vestibular problem is the root of dyspraxia. I'm sure that's not right. In the case of my son, it turned out to be a huge component, consistent with his particular difficulty with spatial processing. Every case is different and requires a long, frustrating search, a trial-and-error experiment in which your baby is the guinea pig. For my son, the vestibular component turned out to be prominent and, even more importantly, fixable.

* * *

In third grade we began astronaut training.

Astronaut training is literally training developed by NASA to help astronauts maintain good spatial orientation in zero gravity. It revs up the vestibular signal and forces the brain to process that unaccustomed information. It's increasingly popular in occupational therapy for patients, often elderly ones, who need to tune up their balance. For us it meant daily exercises along with all the other movement therapies. The exercises seemed trivial. Tilting the head certain ways, spinning so many times this way and that, touching one toe and then the other. Every exercise had a cute name. Robot zapping. Passing the star. As cutesy as they sounded and trivial as they seemed, they were powerful medicine. We were warned. My son shouldn't do them close to bedtime or the dizziness would disturb his sleep. Sometimes I did the exercises with him, and then for the rest of the day my head would spin. Once a week at the clinic he would get on a tilt board and give his inner ear an extra workout.

The astronaut training seemed to put a missing piece in place. Suddenly he began to understand the space around him. The other therapies, that had spun their wheels in the mud for two years, now suddenly caught traction and began to work. He began to learn how to move more fluidly, and he crashed into walls and people a whole lot less often.

We bought a trampoline, a welcome addition to the therapy because it was more like a game than a chore. Our pediatrician looked at us squint-eyed and said, "Are you serious? You know that, as a pediatrician, I'm not supposed to sanction that!" But with proper safeguards, such as pads and nets, the trampoline is standard gear for the dyspraxic household. My son invented his own game, and if there's any better, more intensive way to exercise personal space, I'd like to know what it is. He strung bungee cords across the trampoline at about waist height, three cords cutting the circular space into six pie pieces. He also loosed several beach balls into the mix. Then he'd jump over the cords, from one pie partition to the next, trying to avoid touching the cords with any part of his body while at the same time twisting and turning to dodge the beach balls, which were jumping crazily all directions. If he could get around the circle through all six partitions without touching or hitting anything, then he'd win. Now *that's* a personal space workout.

Within the first months of astronaut training, strange, miraculous things began to happen. He could suddenly read a lot more comfortably. He moved better as he walked and ran. He sat better. He held a pencil better. He had no trouble navigating the personal space of other people. He was confident in a crowd of other kids and fit in seamlessly. He became one of the most popular kids, because he was friendly, kind, and open. We had a lot less spilled milk at the table. Over the course of third grade, he caught up to the class in all his subjects. He no longer had that weird, unbridgeable gap between what he knew in his mind and what he could do with his hands and body.

I don't want to say that vestibular training and a trampoline solved all his problems. He had a lot of other interventions, too. For example, he did exercises to strengthen his core muscles. He also had daily practice juggling two tasks at the same time, such as running on a treadmill while tossing beanbags. And even with years of intensive therapy, he will never be that super-coordinated athlete, and his handwriting will probably always be messy. Dyspraxia is a lifelong condition.[1]

Maybe that lifelong struggle will give him a perspective on self-improvement. You should always strive to be better. It has certainly already given him a uniquely empathetic view of other people. Sometimes the things we call disabilities can be a source of strength instead of weakness. Like in any resistance training, you build up your strength by pushing against an obstacle.

A lot of other lessons could come out of this story. Always fight for your child. The system can turn against you, and then you have to fight back as hard as you can and look for the right people to help you. Another lesson might be this: the real enemy is ignorance. Especially in the case of dyspraxia, the invisible disability, people look right at it and see something else. They see something stigmatizing. That's why I try to speak openly about my son's case. Parents and teachers should know what dyspraxia is and what it can do to a child.

But among all the many lessons, one of them has a particular significance for me as a scientist. My son's story, as much as it is about anything, is about the devastating importance of personal space. Personal space is a scaffold that supports everything we do. Weaken that scaffold, especially in childhood, when basic skills are still developing, and the consequences ripple into all aspects of life.

Here are some of the many facets of personal space illustrated by my son's story:

Personal space is a margin of safety. You avoid collisions by keeping track of where objects are and how they're moving around you. Without a good margin of safety, you crash into things—or let them crash into you. You end up bruised and with broken bones.

Beyond safety, personal space affects all your movements with respect to the objects near you. Reaching, grasping, sitting at a desk, walking through a room—everything becomes a special challenge without a good sense of nearby space.

Personal space plays a unique role in tool use. Tools may even be an evolutionary outgrowth of personal space. To be able to use a tool, you need to extend your personal space around the tool, in effect incorporating the object into your body schema. You intuitively judge the space around the tool as if it were an extension of your own hand. Without a well-organized personal space, what chance do you have to manage a pen, or a fork and knife?

Personal space has a hidden impact on education. Mathematics, the most abstract branch of human thought, grows developmentally out of spatial processing. If nothing else, it's mighty useful to be able to point and count accurately when you start out learning math. And it's useful to read and write the numbers. How can you learn to read and write if you have trouble with the spatial relationships of letters, words, or even the whole darn book with respect to yourself? All the basics of education are at risk of derailment.

And yet the most devastating consequence may be the social consequence. Personal space is the fundamental scaffold of human interaction. That mechanism works mostly outside of consciousness, shaping our judgments of other people and our interpersonal behavior. As long as it works correctly, we don't even know it's there. When it goes wrong, that's when people can get blamed, accused, and rejected, all the way to the level of courtroom drama. That, to me, is the most bizarre aspect of the story. From a failure of personal space and a few unfriendly eyes came a total breakdown of social acceptance, a bullied child, a family in crisis for months, and a court case.

I studied personal space in the lab. For years, I studied the brain basis of it. But I was in no way prepared for its full human dimensions.

It's as if I had studied the skeletal anatomy of tigers all my life, and then, hiking in an Indonesian jungle, come face to face with a live one. "Wow," I think to myself. "*Now* what do I do?"

I hope this book has conveyed some sense of the reality of personal space, not just as a fascinating scientific topic, but as a vast invisible presence affecting all of us all the time.

Notes

Chapter 2

1. Strauss, H. (1929). Das Zusammenschrecken. *Journal für Psychologie und Neurologie* 39: 111–231.
2. Landis, C., and Hunt, W.A. (1939). *The Startle Pattern*. New York: Farrar and Rinehart.
3. Davis, M. (1984). The mammalian startle response. In: *Neural Mechanisms of Startle*. Edited by R.C. Eaton. New York: Plenum Press.
4. Koch, M. (1999). The neurobiology of startle. *Prog. Neurobiol.* 59: 107–128.
5. Fendt, M., Li, L., and Yeomans, J.S. (2001). Brain stem circuits mediating prepulse inhibition of the startle reflex. *Psychopharmacology (Berl.)* 156: 216–224.
6. Davis, M., Falls, W., Campeau, S., and Kim, M. (1993). Fear-potentiated startle: a neural and pharmacological analysis. *Behav. Brain. Res.* 58:175–198.
7. Grillon, C., and Baas, J. (2003). A review of the modulation of the startle reflex by affective states and its application in psychiatry. *Clin. Neurophysiol.* 114: 1557–1579.

8. Dawson, M.E., Schell, A.M., and Bohmelt, A.H. (2008). *Startle Modification: Implications for Neuroscience, Cognitive Science, and Clinical Science,* 2nd ed. Cambridge, UK: Cambridge University Press.
9. Grillon, C. (2008). Models and mechanisms of anxiety: evidence from startle studies. *Psychopharmacology* 199: 421–437.
10. McTeague, L.M., and Lang, P.J. (2012). The anxiety spectrum and the reflex physiology of defense: from circumscribed fear to broad distress. *Depress Anxiety* 29: 264–281.
11. Grillon, C., Ameli, R., Woods, S.W., Merikangas, K., and Davis, M. (1991). Fear-potentiated startle in humans: effects of anticipatory anxiety on the acoustic blink reflex. *Psychophysiology* 28: 588–595.
12. Lang, P.J., Bradley, M.M., and Cuthbert, B.N. (1990). Emotion, attention, and the startle reflex. *Psychol. Rev.* 97: 377–395.
13. Ehrlichman, H., Brown, S., Zhu, J., and Warrenburg, S. (1995). Startle reflex modulation during exposure to pleasant and unpleasant odors. *Psychophysiology* 32: 150–154.
14. Patrick, C.J., Berthot, B.D., and Moore, J.D. (1996). Diazepam blocks fear-potentiated startle in humans. *J. Abnorm. Psychol.* 105: 89–96.
15. Grillon, C., Ameli, R., Goddard, A., Woods, S.W., and Davis, M. (1994). Baseline and fear-potentiated startle in panic disorder patients. *Biol. Psychiatry* 35: 431–439.
16. Grillon, C., Morgan, C.A., Southwick, S.M., Davis, M., and Charney, D.S. (1996). Baseline startle amplitude and prepulse inhibition in Vietnam veterans with posttraumatic stress disorder. *Psychiatr. Res.* 64: 169–178.

Chapter 3

1. Hediger, H. (1955). *The Psychology and Behavior of Animals in Zoos and Circuses.* Translated by Geoffrey Sircom. London: Butterworths Scientific Publications.
2. Ibid, p. 39.
3. Gross, C.G., and Graziano, M.S.A. (1995). Multiple representations of space in the brain. *The Neuroscientist* 1: 43–50.
4. Wang, R., and Spelke, E. (2002). Human spatial representation: insights from animals. *Trends Cogn. Sci.* 6: 376–382.

5. Burgess, N. (2006). Spatial memory: how egocentric and allocentric combine. *Trends Cogn. Sci.* 10: 551–557.
6. Proulx, M.J., Todorov, O.S., Taylor Aiken, A., and de Sousa, A.A. (2016). Where am I? Who am I? The relation between spatial cognition, social cognition and individual differences in the built environment. *Front. Psychol.* 7: 64. doi: 10.3389/fpsyg.2016.00064
7. Hediger, p. 67
8. Clutton-Brock, J. (1988). *A Natural History of Domesticated Mammals.* Cambridge, UK: Cambridge University Press.
9. Larson, G., and Fuller, D.Q. (2014). The evolution of animal domestication. *Annu. Rev. Ecol. Evol. Syst.* 45: 115–136.
10. Zeder, M.A. (2015). Core questions in domestication research. *Proc. Natl. Acad. Sci. U. S. A.* 112: 3191–3198.
11. Smith, B. (1998). *Moving 'em.* Kamuela, Hawaii: The Graziers Hui Publisher.
12. Hediger, p. 49.

Chapter 4

1. Hall, E. (1966). *The Hidden Dimension.* New York: Anchor Books.
2. Ibid, p. 155.
3. Ibid, p. 150.
4. Ibid, p. 117.
5. Dosey, M.A., and Meisels, M. (1969). Personal space and self-protection. *J. Pers. Soc. Psychol.* 11: 93–97.
6. Hartnett, J.J., Bailey, K.G., and Gibson, F.W., Jr. (1970). Personal space as influenced by sex and type of movement. *J. Psychol.* 76: 139–144.
7. Meisels, M., and Dosey, M.A. (1971). Personal space, anger-arousal, and psychological defense. *J. Pers.* 39: 333–344.
8. Felipe, N.J., and Sommer, R. (1966). Invasions of personal space. *Soc. Probl.* 14: 206–214.
9. Middlemist, R.D., Knowles, E.S., and Matter, C.F. (1976). Personal space invasions in the lavatory: suggestive evidence for arousal. *J. Pers. Soc. Psychol.* 33: 541–546.
10. Bailey, K.G., Hartnett, J.J., and Gibson, F.W. Jr. (1972). Implied threat and the territorial factor in personal space. *Psychol. Rep.* 30: 263–270.

11. Allekian, C.I. (1973). Intrusions of territory and personal space: an anxiety-inducing factor for hospitalized persons—an exploratory study. *Nurs. Res.* 22: 236–241.

12. Brady, A.T., and Walker, M.B. (1978). Interpersonal distance as a function of situationally induced anxiety. *Br. J. Soc. Clin. Psychol.* 17: 127–233.

13. Cavallin, B.A., and Houston, B.K. (1980). Aggressiveness, maladjustment, body experience and the protective function of personal space. *J. Clin. Psychol.* 36: 170–176.

14. Ricci, M.S. (1981). An experiment with personal-space invasion in the nurse-patient relationship and its effects on anxiety. *Issues Ment. Health Nurs.* 3: 203–218.

15. McElroy, J.C., and Middlemist, R.D. (1983). Personal space, crowding, and the interference model of test anxiety. *Psychol. Rep.* 53: 419–424.

16. Long, G.T. (1984). Psychological tension and closeness to others: stress and interpersonal distance preference. *J. Psychol.* 117: 143–246.

17. Roger, D.B. (1982). Body-image, personal space and self-esteem: preliminary evidence for "focusing" effects. *J. Pers. Assess.* 46: 468–476.

18. Horowitz, M.J., Duff, D.F., and Stratton, L.O. (1964). Body-buffer zone; exploration of personal space. *Arch. Gen. Psychiatry* 11: 651–656.

19. Beck, S.J., and Ollendick, T.H. (1976). Personal space, sex of experimenter, and locus of control in normal and delinquent adolescents. *Psychol. Rep.* 38: 383–387.

20. Edwards, D.J. (1977). Perception of crowding and personal space as a function of locus of control, arousal seeking, sex of experimenter, and sex of subject. *J. Psychol.* 95: 223–229.

21. Latta, R.M. (1978). Relation of status incongruence to personal space. *Pers. Soc. Psychol. Bull.* 4: 143–146.

22. Sanders, J.L., Hakky, U.M., and Brizzolara, M.M. (1985). Personal space amongst Arabs and Americans. *Int. J. Psychol.* 20: 13–17.

23. Sommer, R. (1959). Studies in personal space. *Sociometry* 22: 247–260.

24. Kleck, R., Buck, P.L., Goller, W.L., London, R.S., Pfeiffer, J.R., and Vukcevic, D.P. (1968). Effect of stigmatizing conditions on the use of personal space. *Psychol. Rep.* 23: 111–118.

25. Gottheil, E., Corey, J., and Paredes, A. (1968). Psychological and physical dimensions of personal space. *J. Psychol.* 69: 7–9.
26. Levine, M.E. (1968) Knock before entering: personal space bubbles. 1. *Chart* 65: 58–62.
27. Rodgers, J.A. (1972). Relationship between sociability and personal space: preferences at two times of the day. *Percept. Mot. Skills* 35: 519–526.
28. Pedersen, D.M. (1973). Relationships among self, other, and consensual personal space. *Percept. Mot. Skills* 36: 732–734.
29. Sundstrom, E., and Altman, I. (1976). Interpersonal relationships and personal space: research review and theoretical model. *Hum. Ecol.* 4: 47–67.
30. Melson, G.F. (1976). Determinants of personal space in young children: perception of distance cues. *Percept. Mot. Skills* 43: 107–114.
31. Worchel, S., and Teddlie, C. (1976). The experience of crowding: a two-factor theory. *J. Pers. Soc. Psychol.* 34: 30–40.
32. Hackworth, J.R. (1976). Relationship between spatial density and sensory overload, personal space, and systolic and diastolic blood pressure. *Percept. Mot. Skills* 43: 867–872.
33. Stillman, M.J. (1978). Territoriality and personal space. *Am. J. Nurs.* 78: 1670–1672.
34. Johnson, F.L. (1979). Response to territorial intrusion by nursing home residents. *ANS Adv. Nurs. Sci.* 1: 21–34.
35. Phillips, J.R. (1979). An exploration of perception of body boundary, personal space, and body size in elderly persons. *Percept. Mot. Skills* 48: 299–308.
36. Sanders, J.L., and Suydam, M.M. (1980). Personal space of blind and sighted individuals. *Percept. Mot. Skills* 51: 36.
37. Winogrond, I.R. (1981). A comparison of interpersonal distancing behavior in young and elderly adults. *Int. J. Aging Hum. Dev.* 13: 53–60.
38. Meisenhelder, J.B. (1982). Boundaries of personal space. *Image* 14: 16–19.
39. Burgess, J.W., and McMurphy, D. (1982). The development of proxemic spacing behavior: children's distances to surrounding playmates and adults change between 6 months and 5 years of age. *Dev. Psychobiol.* 15: 557–567.
40. Hayduk, L.A. (1983). Personal space: where we now stand. *Psychol. Bull.* 94: 293–335.

41. Wormith, J.S. (1984). Personal space of incarcerated offenders. *J. Clin. Psychol.* 40: 815–826.

42. Gard, G.C., Turone, R., Devlin, B. (1985). Social interaction and interpersonal distance in normal and behaviorally disturbed boys. *J. Genet. Psychol.* 146: 189–196.

43. Conigliaro, L., Cullerton, S., Flynn, K.E., and Roeder, S. (1989). Stigmatizing artifacts and their effect on personal space. *Psychol. Rep.* 65: 897–898.

Chapter 5

1. Gross, C.G. (2008). Single neuron studies of inferior temporal cortex. *Neuropsychologia* 46: 841–852.

2. Goll, Y., Atlan, G., and Citri, A. (2015). Attention: the claustrum. *Trends Neurosci.* 38: 486–495.

3. Alexander, G.E., DeLong, M.R., and Strick, P.L. (1986). Parallel organization of functionally segregated circuits linking basal ganglia and cortex. *Annu. Rev. Neurosci.* 9: 357–381.

4. Albin, R.L., Young, A.B., and Penney, J.B. (1989). The functional anatomy of basal ganglia disorders. *Trends Neurosci.* 12: 366–375.

5. DeLong, M.R. (1990). Primate models of movement disorders of basal ganglia origin. *Trends Neurosci.* 13: 281–285.

6. Obeso, J.A., Rodriguez, M.C., and DeLong, M.R. (1997). Basal ganglia pathophysiology. A critical review. *Adv. Neurol.* 74: 3–18.

7. Wichmann, T., DeLong, M.R., Guridi, J., and Obeso, J.A. (2011). Milestones in research on the pathophysiology of Parkinson's disease. *Mov. Disord.* 26: 1032–1041.

8. Alexander, G.E., and DeLong, M.R. (1985). Microstimulation of the primate neostriatum. I. Physiological properties of striatal microexcitable zones. *J. Neurophysiol.* 53: 1401–1416.

9. Crutcher, M.D., and DeLong, M.R. (1984). Single cell studies of the primate putamen. I. Functional organization. *Exp. Brain Res.* 53: 233–243.

10. Graziano, M.S.A., and Gross, C.G. (1993). A bimodal map of space: somatosensory receptive fields in the macaque putamen with corresponding visual receptive fields. *Exp. Brain Res.* 97: 96–109.

11. Luppino, G., Murata, A., Govoni, P., and Matelli, M. (1999). Largely segregated parietofrontal connections linking rostral intraparietal cortex (areas AIP and VIP) and the ventral premotor cortex (areas F5 and F4). *Exp. Brain Res.* 128: 181–187.

12. Matelli, M., and Luppino, G. (2001). Parietofrontal circuits for action and space perception in the macaque monkey. *Neuroimage* 14: S27–S32.

13. Gharbawie, O.A., Stepniewska, I., and Kaas, J.H. (2011). Cortical connections of functional zones in posterior parietal cortex and frontal cortex motor regions in new world monkeys. *Cereb. Cortex* 21: 1981–2002.

14. Kaas, J.H., Gharbawie, O.A., and Stepniewska, I. (2013). Cortical networks for ethologically relevant behaviors in primates. *Am. J. Primatol.* 75: 407–414.

15. Hyvarinen, J., and Poranen, A. (1974). Function of the parietal associative area 7 as revealed from cellular discharges in alert monkeys. *Brain* 97: 673–692.

16. Leinonen, L., Hyvarinen, J., Nyman, G., and Linnankoski, I. (1979). I. Functional properties of neurons in the lateral part of associative area 7 in awake monkeys. *Exp. Brain Res.* 34: 299–320.

17. Leinonen, L., and Nyman, G. (1979). II. Functional properties of cells in anterolateral part of area 7 associative face area of awake monkeys. *Exp. Brain Res.* 34: 321–333.

18. Hyvarinen, J. (1981). Regional distribution of functions in parietal association area 7 of the monkey. *Brain Res.* 206: 287–303.

19. Colby, C.L., Duhamel, J.R., and Goldberg, M.E. (1993). Ventral intraparietal area of the macaque: anatomic location and visual response properties. *J. Neurophysiol.* 69: 902–914.

20. Schaafsma, S.J., and Duysens, J. (1996). Neurons in the ventral intraparietal area of awake macaque monkey closely resemble neurons in the dorsal part of the medial superior temporal area in their responses to optic flow patterns. *J. Neurophysiol.* 76: 4056–4068.

21. Duhamel, J.R., Bremmer, F., Ben Hamed, S., and Graf, W. (1997). Spatial invariance of visual receptive fields in parietal cortex neurons. *Nature* 389: 845–848.

22. Duhamel, J.R., Colby, C.L., and Goldberg, M.E. (1998). Ventral intraparietal area of the macaque: congruent visual and somatic response properties. *J. Neurophysiol.* 79: 126–136.

23. Bremmer, F., Duhamel, J.R., Ben Hamed, S., and Graf, W. (2002). Heading encoding in the macaque ventral intraparietal area (VIP). *Eur. J. Neurosci.* 16: 1554–1568.

24. Cooke, D.F., Taylor, C.S.R., Moore, T., and Graziano, M.S.A. (2003). Complex movements evoked by microstimulation of the ventral intraparietal area. *Proc. Natl. Acad. Sci. U.S.A.* 100: 6163–6168.

25. Zhang, T., Heuer, H.W., and Britten, K. H. (2004). Parietal area VIP neuronal responses to heading stimuli are encoded in head-centered coordinates. *Neuron* 42: 993–1001.

26. Avillac, M., Ben Hamed, S., and Duhamel, J.R. (2007). Multisensory integration in the ventral intraparietal area of the macaque monkey. *J. Neurosci.* 27: 1922–1932.

27. Zhang, T., and Britten, K.H. (2011). Parietal area VIP causally influences heading perception during pursuit eye movements. *J. Neurosci.* 31: 2569–2575.

28. Bremmer, F., Schlack, A., Kaminiarz, A., and Hoffmann, K.P. (2013). Encoding of movement in near extrapersonal space in primate area VIP. *Front. Behav. Neurosci.* 7: 8. doi: 10.3389/fnbeh.2013.00008

29. Chen, A., Deangelis, G.C., and Angelaki, D.E. (2013). Functional specializations of the ventral intraparietal area for multisensory heading discrimination. *J. Neurosci.* 33: 3567–3581.

30. Guipponi, O., Wardak, C., Ibarrola, D., Comte, J.C., Sappey-Marinier, D., Pinède, S., and Ben Hamed, S. (2013). Multimodal convergence within the intraparietal sulcus of the macaque monkey. *J. Neurosci.* 33: 4128–4139.

31. Kaminiarz, A., Schlack, A., Hoffmann, K.P., Lappe, M., and Bremmer, F. (2014). Visual selectivity for heading in the macaque ventral intraparietal area. *J. Neurophysiol.* 112: 2470–2480.

32. Schlack, A., Sterbing-D'Angelo, S.J., Hartung, K., Hoffmann, K.P., and Bremmer, F. (2005). Multisensory space representations in the macaque ventral intraparietal area (VIP). *J. Neurosci.* 25: 4616–4625.

33. Bremmer, F., Klam, F., Duhamel, J.R., Ben Hamed, S., and Graf, W. (2002). Visual-vestibular interactive responses in the macaque ventral intraparietal area (VIP). *Eur. J. Neurosci.* 16: 1569–1586.

34. Gabel, S.F., Misslisch, H., Gielen, C.C., and Duysens, J. (2002). Responses of neurons in area VIP to self-induced and external visual motion. *Exp. Brain Res.* 147: 520–528.

35. Klam, F., and Graf, W. (2006). Discrimination between active and passive head movements by macaque ventral and medial intraparietal cortex neurons. *J. Physiol.* 574: 367–386.

36. Chen, A., DeAngelis, G.C., and Angelaki, D.E. (2011). A comparison of vestibular spatiotemporal tuning in macaque parieto-insular vestibular cortex, ventral intraparietal area, and medial superior temporal area. *J. Neurosci.* 31: 3082–3094.

37. Rizzolatti, G., Scandolara, C., Matelli, M., and Gentilucci, M. (1981). Afferent properties of periarcuate neurons in macaque monkeys. II. Visual responses. *Behav. Brain Res.* 2: 147–163.

38. Gentilucci, M., Scandolara, C., Pigarev, I.N., and Rizzolatti, G. (1983). Visual responses in the postarcuate cortex (area 6) of the monkey that are independent of eye position. *Exp. Brain Res.* 50: 464–468.

39. Gentilucci, M., Fogassi, L., Luppino, G., Matelli, M., Camarda, R., and Rizzolatti, G. (1988). Functional organization of inferior area 6 in the macaque monkey. I. Somatotopy and the control of proximal movements. *Exp. Brain Res.* 71: 475–490.

40. Fogassi, L., Gallese, V., di Pellegrino, G., Fadiga, L., Gentilucci, M., Luppino, G., Matelli, M., Pedotti, A., and Rizzolatti, G. (1992). Space coding by premotor cortex. *Exp. Brain Res.* 89: 686–690.

41. Fogassi, L., Gallese, V., Fadiga, L., Luppino, G., Matelli, M., and Rizzolatti, G. (1996). Coding of peripersonal space in inferior premotor cortex (area F4). *J. Neurophysiol.* 76: 141–157.

42. Matelli, M., Luppino, G., and Rizzolatti, G. (1985). Patterns of cytochrome oxidase activity in the frontal agranular cortex of the macaque monkey. *Behav. Brain Res.* 18: 125–136.

43. Graziano, M.S.A., and Gandhi, S. (2000). Location of the polysensory zone in the precentral gyrus of anesthetized monkeys. *Exp. Brain Res.* 135: 259–266.

Chapter 6

1. Rizzolatti, G., Scandolara, C., Matelli, M., and Gentilucci, M. (1981). Afferent properties of periarcuate neurons in macaque monkeys. II. Visual responses. *Behav. Brain Res.* 2: 147–163.

2. Gentilucci, M., Scandolara, C., Pigarev, I.N., and Rizzolatti, G. (1983). Visual responses in the postarcuate cortex (area 6) of the monkey that are independent of eye position. *Exp. Brain Res.* 50: 464–468.

3. Gentilucci, M., Fogassi, L., Luppino, G., Matelli, M., Camarda, R., and Rizzolatti, G. (1988). Functional organization of inferior area 6 in the macaque monkey. I. Somatotopy and the control of proximal movements. *Exp. Brain Res.* 71: 475–490.

4. Graziano, M.S.A., Yap, G.S., and Gross, C.G. (1994). Coding of visual space by pre-motor neurons. *Science* 266: 1054–1057.

5. Graziano, M.S.A., Hu, X.T., and Gross, C.G. (1997). Coding the locations of objects in the dark. *Science* 277: 239–241.

6. Graziano, M.S.A., Hu, X.T., and Gross, C.G. (1997). Visuo-spatial properties of ventral premotor cortex. *J. Neurophysiol.* 77: 2268–2292.

7. Graziano, M.S.A., and Gross, C.G. (1998). Visual responses with and without fixation: neurons in premotor cortex encode spatial locations independently of eye position. *Exp. Brain Res.* 118: 373–380.

8. Graziano, M.S.A. (1999). Where is my arm? The relative role of vision and proprioception in the neuronal representation of limb position. *Proc. Natl. Acad. Sci. U.S.A.* 96: 10418–10421.

9. Graziano, M.S.A., Reiss, L.A.J., and Gross, C.G. (1999). A neuronal representation of the location of nearby sounds. *Nature* 397: 428–430.

10. Graziano, M.S.A., Cooke, D.F., and Taylor, C.S.R. (2000). Coding the location of the arm by sight. *Science* 290: 1782–1786.

11. Graziano, M.S.A., and Gandhi, S. (2000). Location of the polysensory zone in the precentral gyrus of anesthetized monkeys. *Exp. Brain Res.* 135: 259–266.

12. Graziano, M.S.A., Alisharan, S.A., Hu, X., and Gross, C.G. (2002). The clothing effect: tactile neurons in the precentral gyrus do not respond to the touch of the familiar primate chair. *Proc. Natl. Acad. Sci. U.S.A.* 99: 11930–11933.

13. Gardener, J. (1972) *The Sunlight Dialogues.* New York: Alfred A. Knopf.

14. Bremmer, F., Klam, F., Duhamel, J.R., Ben Hamed, S., and Graf, W. (2002). Visual-vestibular interactive responses in the macaque ventral intraparietal area (VIP). *Eur. J. Neurosci.* 16: 1569–1586.

15. Klam, F., and Graf, W. (2006). Discrimination between active and passive head movements by macaque ventral and medial intraparietal cortex neurons. *J. Physiol.* 574: 367–386.

16. Chen, A., DeAngelis, G.C., and Angelaki, D.E. (2011). A comparison of vestibular spatiotemporal tuning in macaque parieto-insular vestibular cortex, ventral intraparietal area, and medial superior temporal area. *J. Neurosci.* 31: 3082–3094.

17. Blauert, J. (1997). *Spatial Hearing: The Psychophysics of Human Sound Localization.* Translated by J. S. Allen. Cambridge, MA: MIT Press.

18. Supa, M., Cotzin, M., and Dallenbach, K. M. (1944). "Facial vision"—the perception of obstacles by the blind. *Am. J. Psychol.* 57: 133–183.

19. Cotzin, M., and Dallenbach, K.M. (1950). "Facial vision"—the role of pitch and loudness in the location of obstacles by the blind. *Am. J. Psychol.* 63: 485–515.

20. Kolarik, A.J., Cirstea, S., Pardhan, S., and Moore, B.C.J. (2014). A summary of research investigating echolocation abilities of blind and sighted humans. *Hearing Res.* 310: 60–68.

21. Dahl, R. (1977). *The Wonderful Story of Henry Sugar, and Six More.* London: Jonathan Cape.

22. Kusek, K. (1998). How you find your lover's lips in the dark. *Glamour Magazine*, March, p. 77.

23. Andersen, R.A., and Mountcastle, V.B. (1983). The influence of the angle of gaze upon the excitability of the light-sensitive neurons of the posterior parietal cortex. *J. Neurosci.* 3: 532–548.

24. Andersen, R.A., Essick, G.K., and Siegel, R.M. (1985). Encoding of spatial location by posterior parietal neurons. *Science* 230: 456–458.

25. Zipser, D., and Andersen, R.A. (1988). A back-propagation programmed network that simulates response properties of a subset of posterior parietal neurons. *Nature* 311: 679–684.

26. Andersen, R.A., Bracewell, R.M., Barash, S., Gnadt, J.W., and Fogassi, L. (1990). Eye-position effects on visual, memory, and saccade-related activity in areas LIP and 7a of macaque. *J. Neurosci.* 10: 1176–1196.

27. Brotchie, P.R., Andersen, R.A., Snyder, L.H., and Goodman, S.J. (1995). Head position signals used by parietal neurons to encode locations of visual stimuli. *Nature* 375: 232–235.

28. Stricanne, B., Andersen, R.A., and Mazzoni, P. (1996). Eye-centered, head-centered, and intermediate coding of remembered sound locations in area LIP. *J. Neurophysiol.* 76: 2071–2076.

29. Snyder, L.H., Grieve, K.L., Brotchie, P., and Andersen, R.A. (1998). Separate body- and world-referenced representations of visual space in parietal cortex. *Nature* 394: 887–891.
30. Batista, A.P., Buneo, C.A., Snyder, L.H., and Andersen, R.A. (1999). Reach plans in eye-centered coordinates. *Science* 285: 257–260.
31. Xing, J., and Andersen, R.A. (2000). Models of the posterior parietal cortex which perform multimodal integration and represent space in several coordinate frames. *J. Cogn. Neurosci.* 12: 601–614.
32. Cohen, Y.E., and Andersen, R.A. (2000). Reaches to sounds encoded in an eye-centered reference frame. *Neuron* 27: 647–652.
33. Buneo, C.A., Jarvis, M.R., Batista, A.P., and Andersen, R.A. (2002). Direct visuomotor transformations for reaching. *Nature* 416: 632–636.
34. Pigarev, I.N., and Rodionova, E.I. (1988). Neurons with visual receptive fields independent of the position of the eyes in cat parietal cortex. *Sensornie Sistemi* 2: 245–254.
35. Galletti, C., Battaglini, P.P., and Fattori, P. (1993). Parietal neurons encoding spatial locations in craniotopic coordinates. *Exp. Brain Res.* 96: 221–229.
36. Duhamel, J.R., Bremmer, F., Ben Hamed, S., and Graf, W. (1997). Spatial invariance of visual receptive fields in parietal cortex neurons. *Nature* 389: 845–848.
37. Gross, C.G., and Graziano, M.S.A. (1995). Multiple representations of space in the brain. *The Neuroscientist* 1: 43–50.
38. Fogassi, L., Gallese, V., di Pellegrino, G., Fadiga, L., Gentilucci, M., Luppino, G., Matelli, M., Pedotti, A., and Rizzolatti, G. (1992). Space coding by premotor cortex. *Exp. Brain Res.* 89: 686–690.
39. Fogassi, L., Gallese, V., Fadiga, L., Luppino, G., Matelli, M., and Rizzolatti, G. (1996). Coding of peripersonal space in inferior premotor cortex (area F4). *J. Neurophysiol.* 76: 141–157.

Chapter 7

1. Robinson, D.A., and Fuchs, A.F. (1969). Eye movements evoked by stimulation of frontal eye fields. *J. Neurophysiol.* 32: 637–648.
2. Bruce, C.J., Goldberg, M.E., Bushnell, M.C., and Stanton, G.B. (1985). Primate frontal eye fields. II. Physiological and

anatomical correlates of electrically evoked eye movements. *J. Neurophysiol.* 54: 714–734.

3. Dassonville, P., Schlag, J., and Schlag-Rey, M. (1992). The frontal eye field provides the goal of saccadic eye movement. *Exp. Brain Res.* 89: 300–310.

4. Gottlieb, J.P., Bruce, C.J., and MacAvoy, M.G. (1993). Smooth eye movements elicited by microstimulation in the primate frontal eye field. *J. Neurophysiol.* 69: 786–799.

5. Fujii, N., Mushiake, H., and Tanji, J. (1998). Intracortical microstimulation of bilateral frontal eye field. *J. Neurophysiol.* 79: 2240–2244.

6. Tehovnik, E.J., Slocum, W.M., and Schiller, P.H. (1999). Behavioural conditions affecting saccadic eye movements elicited electrically from the frontal lobes of primates. *Eur. J. Neurosci.* 11: 2431–2443.

7. Knight, T.A., and Fuchs, A.F. (2007). Contribution of the frontal eye field to gaze shifts in the head-unrestrained monkey: effects of microstimulation. *J. Neurophysiol.* 97: 618–634.

8. Moore, T., and Fallah, M. (2001). Control of eye movements and spatial attention. *Proc. Natl. Acad. Sci. U.S.A.* 98: 1273–1276.

9. Moore, T., and Armstrong, K.M. (2003). Selective gating of visual signals by microstimulation of frontal cortex. *Nature* 421: 370–373.

10. Moore, T., and Fallah, M. (2004). Microstimulation of the frontal eye field and its effects on covert spatial attention. *J. Neurophysiol.* 91: 152–162.

11. Armstrong, K.M., and Moore, T. (2007). Rapid enhancement of visual cortical response discriminability by microstimulation of the frontal eye field. *Proc. Natl. Acad. Sci. U.S.A.* 104: 9499–9504.

12. Schafer, R.J., and Moore, T. (2007). Attention governs action in the primate frontal eye field. *Neuron* 56: 541–551.

13. Armstrong, K.M., Chang, M.H., and Moore, T. (2009). Selection and maintenance of spatial information by frontal eye field neurons. *J. Neurosci.* 29: 15621–15629.

14. Noudoost, B., Clark, K.L., and Moore, T. (2014). A distinct contribution of the frontal eye field to the visual representation of saccadic targets. *J. Neurosci.* 34: 3687–3698.

15. Fritsch, G., and Hitzig, E. (1870). Ueber die elektrishe Erregbarkeit des Grosshirns. Translated by G. von Bonin. In: *The Cerebral*

Cortex. Edited by W. W. Nowinski. Springfield, IL: Thomas, pp. 73–96.

16. Graziano, M.S.A. (2008). *The Intelligent Movement Machine.* New York: Oxford University Press.

17. Penfield, W., and Boldrey, E. (1937). Somatic motor and sensory representation in the cerebral cortex of man as studied by electrical stimulation. *Brain* 60: 389–443.

18. Penfield, W., and Rasmussen, T. (1950). *The Cerebral Cortex of Man. A Clinical Study of Localization of Function.* New York: Macmillan.

19. Ferrier, D. (1874). Experiments on the brain of monkeys—No. 1. *Proc. R. Soc. Lond.* 23: 409–430.

20. Beevor, C., and Horsley, V. (1887). A minute analysis (experimental) of the various movements produced by stimulating in the monkey different regions of the cortical centre for the upper limb, as defined by Professor Ferrier. *Phil. Trans. R. Soc. Lond. B* 178: 153–167.

21. Asanuma, H., and Ward, J.E. (1971). Pattern of contraction of distal forelimb muscles produced by intracortical stimulation in cats. *Brain Res.* 27: 97–109.

22. Huang, C.S., Hiraba, H., Murray, G.M., and Sessle, B.J. (1989). Topographical distribution and functional properties of cortically induced rhythmical jaw movements in the monkey (*Macaca fascicularis*). *J. Neurophysiol.* 61: 635–650.

23. Freedman, E.G., Stanford, T.R., and Sparks, D.L. (1996). Combined eye-head gaze shifts produced by electrical stimulation of the superior colliculus in rhesus monkeys. *J. Neurophysiol.* 76: 927–952.

24. Stanford, T.R., Freedman, E.G., and Sparks, D.L. (1996). Site and parameters of microstimulation: evidence for independent effects on the properties of saccades evoked from the primate superior colliculus. *J. Neurophysiol.* 76: 3360–3381.

25. Martinez-Trujillo, J.C., Wang, H., and Crawford, J.D. (2003). Electrical stimulation of the supplementary eye fields in the head-free macaque evokes kinematically normal gaze shifts. *J. Neurophysiol.* 89: 2961–2974.

26. Chen, L.L., and Walton, M.M. (2005). Head movement evoked by electrical stimulation in the supplementary eye field of the rhesus monkey. *J. Neurophysiol.* 94: 4502–4519.

27. Graziano, M.S.A., Taylor, C.S.R., and Moore, T. (2002). Complex movements evoked by microstimulation of precentral cortex. *Neuron* 34: 841–851.
28. Graziano, M.S.A., Cooke, D.F., Taylor, C.S.R., and Moore, T. (2004) Distribution of hand location in monkeys during spontaneous behavior. *Exp. Brain Res.* 155: 30–36.
29. Cooke, D.F., and Graziano, M.S.A. (2004). Sensorimotor integration in the precentral gyrus: polysensory neurons and defensive movements. *J. Neurophysiol.* 91: 1648–1660.
30. Graziano, M.S.A., Patel, K.T., and Taylor, C.S.R. (2004). Mapping from motor cortex to biceps and triceps altered by elbow angle. *J. Neurophysiol.* 92: 395–407.
31. Cooke, D.F., and Graziano, M.S.A. (2004). Super-flinchers and nerves of steel: defensive movements altered by chemical manipulation of a cortical motor area. *Neuron* 43: 585–593.
32. Graziano, M.S.A., Aflalo, T., and Cooke, D.F. (2005). Arm movements evoked by electrical stimulation in the motor cortex of monkeys. *J. Neurophysiol.* 94: 4209–4223.
33. Graziano, M.S.A. (2006). The organization of behavioral repertoire in motor cortex. *Annu. Rev. Neurosci.* 29: 105–134.
34. Aflalo, T.N., and Graziano, M.S.A. (2006). Partial tuning of motor cortex neurons to final posture in a free-moving paradigm. *Proc. Natl. Acad. Sci. U.S.A.* 103: 2909–2914.
35. Aflalo, T.N., and Graziano, M.S.A. (2006). Possible origins of the complex topographic organization of motor cortex: reduction of a multidimensional space onto a 2-dimensional array. *J. Neurosci.* 26: 6288–6297.
36. Graziano, M.S.A., and Aflalo, T.N. (2007). Mapping behavioral repertoire onto the cortex. *Neuron* 56: 239–251.
37. Aflalo, T.N., and Graziano, M.S.A. (2007). Relationship between unconstrained arm movement and single neuron firing in the macaque motor cortex. *J. Neurosci.* 27: 2760–2780.
38. Brecht, M., Schneider, M., Sakmann, B., and Margrie, T.W. (2004). Whisker movements evoked by stimulation of single pyramidal cells in rat motor cortex. *Nature* 427: 704–710.
39. Haiss, F., and Schwarz, C. (2005). Spatial segregation of different modes of movement control in the whisker representation of rat primary motor cortex. *J. Neurosci.* 25: 1579–1587.

40. Stepniewska, I., Fang, P.C., and Kaas, J.H. (2005). Microstimulation reveals specialized subregions for different complex movements in posterior parietal cortex of prosimian galagos. *Proc. Natl. Acad. Sci. U.S.A.* 102: 4878–4883.

41. Cramer, N.P., and Keller, A. (2006). Cortical control of a whisking central pattern generator. *J. Neurophysiol.* 96: 209–217.

42. Ethier, C., Brizzi, L., Darling, W.G., and Capaday, C. (2006). Linear summation of cat motor cortex outputs. *J. Neurosci.* 26: 5574–5581.

43. Ramanathan, D., Conner, J.M., and Tuszynski, M.H. (2006). A form of motor cortical plasticity that correlates with recovery of function after brain injury. *Proc. Natl. Acad. Sci. U.S.A.* 103: 11370–11375.

44. Stepniewska, I., Fang, P.C., and Kaas, J.H. (2009). Organization of the posterior parietal cortex in galagos: I. Functional zones identified by microstimulation. *J. Comp. Neurol.* 517: 765–782.

45. Stepniewska, I., Friedman, R.M., Gharbawie, O.A., Cerkevich, C.M., Roe, A.W., and Kaas, J.H. (2011). Optical imaging in galagos reveals parietal-frontal circuits underlying motor behavior. *Proc. Natl. Acad. Sci. U.S.A.* 108: E725–E732.

46. Gharbawie, O.A., Stepniewska, I., and Kaas, J.H. (2011). Cortical connections of functional zones in posterior parietal cortex and frontal cortex motor regions in New World monkeys. *Cereb. Cortex* 21: 1981–2002.

47. Gharbawie, O.A. Stepniewska, I., Qi, H., and Kaas, J.H. (2011). Multiple parietal-frontal pathways mediate grasping in macaque monkeys. *J. Neurosci.* 31: 11660–11677.

48. Cooke, D.F., Padberg, J., Zahner, T., and Krubitzer, L. (2012). The functional organization and cortical connections of motor cortex in squirrels. *Cereb. Cortex* 22: 1959–1978.

49. Harrison, T.C., Ayling, O.G., and Murphy, T.H. (2012). Distinct cortical circuit mechanisms for complex forelimb movement and motor map topography. *Neuron* 74: 397–409.

50. Isogai, F., Kato, T., Fujimoto, M., Toi, S., Oka, A., Adachi, T., Maeda, Y., Morimoto, T., Yoshida, A., and Masuda, Y. (2012). Cortical area inducing chewing-like rhythmical jaw movements and its connections with thalamic nuclei in guinea pigs. *Neurosci. Res.* 74: 239–247.

51. Overduin, S.A., d'Avella, A., Carmena, J.M., and Bizzi, E. (2012). Microstimulation activates a handful of muscle synergies. *Neuron* 76: 1071–1077.
52. Bonazzi, L., Viaro, R., Lodi, E., Canto, R., Bonifazzi, C., and Franchi, G. (2013). Complex movement topography and extrinsic space representation in the rat forelimb motor cortex as defined by long-duration intracortical microstimulation. *J. Neurosci.* 33: 2097–2107.
53. Brown, A.R., and Teskey, G.C. (2014). Motor cortex is functionally organized as a set of spatially distinct representations for complex movements. *J. Neurosci.* 34: 13574–13585.
54. Budri, M., Lodi, E., and Franchi, G. (2014). Sensorimotor restriction affects complex movement topography and reachable space in the rat motor cortex. *Front. Syst. Neurosci.* 8: 231. doi: 10.3389/fnsys.2014.00231
55. Desmurget, M., Richard, N., Harquel, S., Baraduc, P., Szathmari, A., Mottolese, C., and Sirigu, A. (2014). Neural representations of ethologically relevant hand/mouth synergies in the human precentral gyrus. *Proc. Natl. Acad. Sci. U.S.A.* 111: 5718–5722.
56. Overduin, S.A., d'Avella, A., Carmena, J.M., and Bizzi, E. (2014). Muscle synergies evoked by microstimulation are preferentially encoded during behavior. *Front. Comput. Neurosci.* 8: 20. doi: 10.3389/fncom.2014.00020
57. Stepniewska, I., Gharbawie, O.A., Burish, M.J., and Kaas, J.H. (2014). Effects of muscimol inactivations of functional domains in motor, premotor, and posterior parietal cortex on complex movements evoked by electrical stimulation. *J. Neurophysiol.* 111: 1100–1119.
58. Graziano, M.S.A. (2015). Ethological action maps: a paradigm shift for the motor cortex. *Trends Cogn. Sci.* 20: 121–132.

Chapter 8

1. Graziano, M.S.A., Taylor, C.S.R., and Moore, T. (2002). Complex movements evoked by microstimulation of precentral cortex. *Neuron* 34: 841–851.
2. Cooke, D.F., and Graziano, M.S.A. (2004). Sensorimotor integration in the precentral gyrus: polysensory neurons and defensive movements. *J. Neurophysiol.* 91: 1648–1660.

3. Cooke, D.F., and Graziano, M.S.A. (2003). Defensive movements evoked by air puff in monkeys. *J. Neurophysiol.* 90: 3317–3329.

4. Gentilucci, M., Fogassi, L., Luppino, G., Matelli, M., Camarda, R., and Rizzolatti, G. (1988). Functional organization of inferior area 6 in the macaque monkey. I. Somatotopy and the control of proximal movements. *Exp. Brain Res.* 71: 475–490.

5. Cooke, D.F., and Graziano, M.S.A. (2004). Super-flinchers and nerves of steel: defensive movements altered by chemical manipulation of a cortical motor area. *Neuron* 43: 585–593.

6. Cooke, D.F., Taylor, C.S.R., Moore, T., and Graziano, M.S.A. (2003). Complex movements evoked by microstimulation of area VIP. *Proc. Natl. Acad. Sci. U.S.A.* 100: 6163–6168.

7. Stepniewska, I., Fang, P.C., and Kaas, J.H. (2005). Microstimulation reveals specialized subregions for different complex movements in posterior parietal cortex of prosimian galagos. *Proc. Natl. Acad. Sci. U.S.A.* 102: 4878–4883.

8. Gharbawie, O.A., Stepniewska, I., and Kaas, J.H. (2011). Cortical connections of functional zones in posterior parietal cortex and frontal cortex motor regions in New World monkeys. *Cereb. Cortex* 21: 1981–2002.

9. Boulanger, M., Bergeron, A., and Guitton, D. (2009). Ipsilateral head and centring eye movements evoked from monkey premotor cortex. *Neuroreport* 20: 669–673.

10. Hocherman, S., and Wise, S.P. (1991). Effects of hand movement path on motor cortical activity in awake, behaving rhesus monkeys. *Exp. Brain Res.* 83: 285–302.

11. Caminiti, R., Ferraina, S., and Johnson, P.B. (1996). The sources of visual information to the primate frontal lobe: a novel role for the superior parietal lobule. *Cereb. Cortex* 6: 319–328.

12. Scott, S.H., Sergio, L.E., and Kalaska, J.F. (1997). Reaching movements with similar hand paths but different arm orientations. II. Activity of individual cells in dorsal premotor cortex and parietal area 5. *J. Neurophysiol.* 78: 2413–2426.

13. Snyder, L.H., Batista, A.P., and Andersen, R.A. (1997). Coding of intention in the posterior parietal cortex. *Nature* 386: 167–170.

14. Messier, J., and Kalaska, J.F. (2000). Covariation of primate dorsal premotor cell activity with direction and amplitude during a memorized-delay reaching task. *J. Neurophysiol.* 84: 152–165.

15. Buneo, C.A., Jarvis, M.R., Batista, A.P., and Andersen, R.A. (2002). Direct visuomotor transformations for reaching. *Nature* 416: 632–636.

16. Cisek, P., and Kalaska, J.F. (2002). Simultaneous encoding of multiple potential reach directions in dorsal premotor cortex. *J. Neurophysiol.* 87: 1149–1154.

17. Batista, A.P., Santhanam, G., Yu, B.M., Ryu, S.I., Afshar, A., and Shenoy, K.V. (2007). Reference frames for reach planning in macaque dorsal premotor cortex. *J. Neurophysiol.* 98: 966–983.

18. Kaufman, M.T., Churchland, M.M., Santhanam, G., Yu, B.M., Afshar, A., Ryu, S.I., and Shenoy, K.V. (2010). Roles of monkey premotor neuron classes in movement preparation and execution. *J. Neurophysiol.* 104: 799–810.

19. Konen, C.S., Mruczek, R.E., Montoya, J.L., and Kastner, S. (2013). Functional organization of human posterior parietal cortex: grasping- and reaching-related activations relative to topographically organized cortex. *J. Neurophysiol.* 109: 2897–9208.

20. Rizzolatti, G., Camarda, R., Fogassi, L., Gentilucci, M., Luppino, G., and Matelli, M. (1988). Functional organization of inferior area 6 in the macaque monkey. II. Area F5 and the control of distal movements. *Exp. Brain Res.* 71: 491–507.

21. Gallese, V., Murata, A., Kaseda, M., Niki, N., and Sakata, H. (1994). Deficit of hand preshaping after muscimol injection in monkey parietal cortex. *Neuroreport* 5: 1525–1529.

22. Sakata, H., Taira, M., Kusunoki, M., Murata, A., and Tanaka, Y. (1997). The TINS Lecture. The parietal association cortex in depth perception and visual control of hand action. *Trends Neurosci.* 20: 350–357.

23. Luppino, G., Murata, A., Govoni, P., and Matelli, M. (1999). Largely segregated parietofrontal connections linking rostral intraparietal cortex (areas AIP and VIP) and the ventral premotor cortex (areas F5 and F4). *Exp. Brain Res.* 128: 181–187.

24. Murata, A., Gallese, V., Luppino, G., Kaseda, M., and Sakata, H. (2000). Selectivity for the shape, size, and orientation of objects for grasping in neurons of monkey parietal area AIP. *J. Neurophysiol.* 83: 2580–2601.

25. Raos, V., Umiltá, M.A., Murata, A., Fogassi, L., and Gallese, V. (2006). Functional properties of grasping-related neurons

in the ventral premotor area F5 of the macaque monkey. *J. Neurophysiol.* 95: 709–729.

26. Colby. C.L. (1998). Action-oriented spatial reference frames in cortex. *Neuron* 20: 15–24.

Chapter 9

1. Brain, W.R. (1941). Visual disorientation with special reference to lesions of the right cerebral hemisphere. *Brain* 263: 244–272.

2. Critchley, M. (1953). *The Parietal Lobes.* New York: Hafner.

3. Halligan, P.W., Fink, G.R., Marshall, J.C., and Vallar, G. (2003). Spatial cognition: evidence from visual neglect. *Trends Cogn. Sci.* 7: 125–133.

4. Corbetta, M. (2014). Hemispatial neglect: clinic, pathogenesis, and treatment. *Semin. Neurol.* 34: 514–523.

5. Vallar, G., and Perani, D. (1986). The anatomy of unilateral neglect after right-hemisphere stroke lesions. A clinical/CT-scan correlation study in man. *Neuropsychologia* 24: 609–622.

6. Mort, D.J., Malhotra, P., Mannan, S.K., Rorden, C., Pambakian, A., Kennard, C., and Husain, M. (2003). The anatomy of visual neglect. *Brain* 126: 1986–1997.

7. Bisiach, E., and Luzzatti, C. (1978). Unilateral neglect of representational space. *Cortex* 14: 129–133.

8. Chen, P., and Goedert, K.M. (2012). Clock drawing in spatial neglect: a comprehensive analysis of clock perimeter, placement, and accuracy. *J. Neuropsychol.* 6: 270–289.

9. Heilman, K.M., and Valenstein, E. (1979). Mechanisms underlying hemispatial neglect *Ann. Neurol.* 5: 166–170.

10. Halligan, P.W, and Marshall, J.C. (1991). Left neglect for near but not far space in man. *Nature* 350: 498–500.

11. Bisiach, E., Perani, D., Vallar, G., and Berti, A. (1986). Unilateral neglect: personal and extra-personal space. *Neuropsychologia* 24: 759–767.

12. Mennemeier, M., Wertman, E., and Heilman, K.M. (1992). Neglect of near peripersonal space: evidence for multidirectional attentional systems in humans. *Brain* 115: 37–50.

13. Cowey, A., Small, M., and Ellis, S. (1994). Visuospatial neglect can be worse in far than in near space. *Neuropsychologia* 32: 1059–1066.

14. Butler, B.C., Eskes, G.A., and Vandorpe, R.A. (2004). Gradients of detection in neglect: comparison of peripersonal and extrapersonal space. *Neuropsychologia* 42: 346–358.

15. Committeri, G., Pitzalis, S., Galati, G., Patria, F., Pelle, G., Sabatini, U., Castriota-Scanderbeg, A., Piccardi, L., Guariglia, C., and Pizzamiglio, L. (2007). Neural bases of personal and extrapersonal neglect in humans. *Brain* 130: 431–441.

16. Grossi, D., Esposito, D., Cuomo, C., Conchiglia, G., and Trojano, L. (2007). Object-based neglect for the near peripersonal space in drawing tasks. *Eur. J. Neurol.* 14: 933–936.

17. Bjoertomt, O., Cowey, A., and Walsh, V. (2009). Near space functioning of the human angular and supramarginal gyri. *J. Neuropsychol.* 3: 31–43.

18. Lane, A.R., Ball, K., Smith, D.T., Schenk, T., and Ellison, A. (2013). Near and far space: understanding the neural mechanisms of spatial attention. *Hum. Brain Mapp.* 34: 356–366.

19. Bartolo, A., Carlier, M., Hassaini, S., Martin, Y., and Coello, Y. (2014). The perception of peripersonal space in right and left brain damage hemiplegic patients. *Front. Hum. Neurosci.* 8: 3. doi: 10.3389/fnhum.2014.00003

20. Nijboer, T.C., Ten Brink, A.F., Kouwenhoven, M., and Visser-Meily, J.M. (2014). Functional assessment of region-specific neglect: are there differential behavioural consequences of peripersonal versus extrapersonal neglect? *Behav. Neurol.* 2014: 526407. doi: 10.1155/2014/526407

21. Nijboer, T.C., Ten Brink, A.F., van der Stoep, N., and Visser-Meily, J.M. (2014). Neglecting posture: differences in balance impairments between peripersonal and extrapersonal neglect. *Neuroreport* 25: 1381–1385.

22. Rapcsak, S.Z., Watson, R.T., and Heilman, K.M. (1987). Hemispace visual field interactions in visual extinction. *J. Neurol. Neurosurg. Psychiatry* 50: 1117–1124.

23. Pellegrino, G., Làdavas, E., and Farne, A. (1997). Seeing where your hands are. *Nature* 388: 730.

24. Làdavas, E., di Pellegrino, G., Farnè, A., and Zeloni, G. (1998). Neuropsychological evidence of an integrated visuotactile representation of peripersonal space in humans. *J. Cogn. Neurosci.* 10: 581–589.

25. Làdavas, E., Zeloni, G., and Farnè, A. (1998). Visual peripersonal space centered on the face in humans. *Brain* 121: 2317–2326.

26. Làdavas, E., Farnè, A., Zeloni, G., and di Pellegrino, G. (2000). Seeing or not seeing where your hands are. *Exp. Brain Res.* 131: 458–467.

27. di Pellegrino, G., and Frassinetti, F. (2000). Direct evidence from parietal extinction of enhancement of visual attention near a visible hand. *Curr. Biol.* 10: 1475–1477.

28. Làdavas, E., Pavani, F., and Farnè, A. (2001). Auditory peripersonal space in humans: a case of auditory-tactile extinction. *Neurocase* 7: 97–103.

29. Farnè, A., and Làdavas, E. (2002). Auditory peripersonal space in humans. *J. Cogn. Neurosci.* 14: 1030–1043.

30. Farnè, A., Demattè, M.L., and Làdavas, E. (2003). Beyond the window: multisensory representation of peripersonal space across a transparent barrier. *Int. J. Psychophysiol.* 50: 51–61.

31. Làdavas, E., and Farnè, A. (2004). Visuo-tactile representation of near-the-body space. *J. Physiol. Paris.* 98: 161–170.

32. Farnè, A., Demattè, M.L., and Làdavas, E. (2005). Neuropsychological evidence of modular organization of the near peripersonal space. *Neurology* 65: 1754–1758.

33. Graziano, M.S.A., Hu, X.T., and Gross, C.G. (1997). Visuo-spatial properties of ventral premotor cortex. *J. Neurophysiol.* 77: 2268–2292.

34. Spence, C., Nicholls, M.E., Gillespie, N., and Driver, J. (1998). Cross-modal links in exogenous covert spatial orienting between touch, audition, and vision. *Percept. Psychophys.* 60: 544–557.

35. Spence, C., Pavani, F., and Driver, J. (2000). Crossmodal links between vision and touch in covert endogenous spatial attention. *J. Exp. Psychol. Hum. Percept. Perform.* 26: 1298–1319.

36. Kennett, S., Eimer, M., Spence, C., and Driver, J. (2001). Tactile-visual links in exogenous spatial attention under different postures: convergent evidence from psychophysics and ERPs. *J. Cogn. Neurosci.* 13: 462–478.

37. Kennett, S., Spence, C., and Driver, J. (2001). Visuo-tactile links in covert exogenous spatial attention remap across changes in unseen hand posture. *Percept. Psychophys.* 64: 1083–1094.

38. Spence, C., Pavani, F., and Driver, J. (2004). Spatial constraints on visual-tactile cross-modal distractor congruency effects. *Cogn. Affect. Behav. Neurosci.* 4: 148–169.

39. Kitagawa, N., and Spence, C. (2005). Investigating the effect of a transparent barrier on the crossmodal congruency effect. *Exp. Brain Res.* 161: 62–71.

40. Brozzoli, C., Cardinali, L., Pavani, F., and Farnè, A. (2010). Action-specific remapping of peripersonal space. *Neuropsychologia* 48: 796–802.

41. Longo, M.R., Musil, J.J., and Haggard, P. (2012). Visuo-tactile integration in personal space. *J. Cogn. Neurosci.* 24: 543–552.

42. van Elk, M., Forget, J., and Blanke, O. (2013). The effect of limb crossing and limb congruency on multisensory integration in peripersonal space for the upper and lower extremities. *Conscious. Cogn.* 22: 545–555.

43. Langerak, R.M., La Mantia, C.L., and Brown, L.E. (2013). Global and local processing near the left and right hands. *Front. Psychol.* 4: 793. doi: 10.3389/fpsyg.2013.00793

44. Van der Biest, L., Legrain, V., Paepe, A.D., and Crombez, G. (2016). Watching what's coming near increases tactile sensitivity: an experimental investigation. *Behav. Brain Res.* 297: 307–314.

45. Noel, J.P., Grivaz, P., Marmaroli, P., Lissek, H., Blanke, O., and Serino, A. (2014). Full body action remapping of peripersonal space: the case of walking. *Neuropsychologia* 70: 375–384.

46. Serino, A., Noel, J.P., Galli, G., Canzoneri, E., Marmaroli, P., Lissek, H., and Blanke O. (2015). Body part–centered and full body–centered peripersonal space representations. *Sci. Rep.* 5: 18603. doi: 10.1038/srep18603

47. Serino, A. (2016). Variability in multisensory responses predicts the self-space. *Trends Cogn. Sci.* 20: 169–170.

48. Dufour, A., and Touzalin, P. (2008). Improved visual sensitivity in the perihand space. *Exp. Brain Res.* 190: 91–98.

49. Li, T., Watter, S., and Sun, H.J. (2011). Differential visual processing for equivalent retinal information from near versus far space. *Neuropsychologia* 49: 3863–3869.

50. Serino, A., Canzoneri, E., and Avenanti, A. (2011). Fronto-parietal areas necessary for a multisensory representation of peripersonal space in humans: an rTMS study. *J. Cogn. Neurosci.* 23: 2956–2967.

51. Canzoneri, E., Magosso, E., and Serino, A. (2012). Dynamic sounds capture the boundaries of peripersonal space representation

in humans. *PLoS One* 7: e44306. doi: 10.1371/journal.pone. 0044306

52. Tseng, P., Yu, J., Tzeng, O.J., Hung, D.L., and Juan, C.H. (2014). Hand proximity facilitates spatial discrimination of auditory tones. *Front. Psychol.* 5: 527. doi: 10.3389/fpsyg.2014.00527

53. Camponogara, I., Komeilipoor, N., and Cesari, P. (2015). When distance matters: perceptual bias and behavioral response for approaching sounds in peripersonal and extrapersonal space. *Neuroscience* 304: 101–108.

54. Finisguerra, A., Canzoneri, E., Serino, A., Pozzo, T., and Bassolino, M. (2015). Moving sounds within the peripersonal space modulate the motor system. *Neuropsychologia* 70: 421–428.

55. Graziano, M.S.A., Yap, G.S., and Gross, C.G. (1994). Coding of visual space by pre-motor neurons. *Science* 266: 1054–1057.

56. de Haan, A.M., Smit, M., Van der Stigchel, S., and Dijkerman, H.C. (2016). Approaching threat modulates visuotactile interactions in peripersonal space. *Exp. Brain Res.* 234: 1875–1884.

57. Graziano, M.S.A., Alisharan, S.A., Hu, X., and Gross, C.G. (2002). The clothing effect: tactile neurons in the precental gyrus do not respond to the touch of the familiar primate chair. *Proc. Natl. Acad. Sci. U.S.A.* 99: 11930–11933.

58. Sambo, C.F., Liang, M., Cruccu, G., and Iannetti, G.D. (2012). Defensive peripersonal space: the blink reflex evoked by hand stimulation is increased when the hand is near the face. *J. Neurophysiol.* 107: 880–889.

59. Sambo, C.F., Forster, B., Williams, S.C., and Iannetti, G.D. (2012). To blink or not to blink: fine cognitive tuning of the defensive peripersonal space. *J. Neurosci.* 32:12921–12927.

60. Coello, Y., Bourgeois, J., and Iachini, T. (2012). Embodied perception of reachable space: how do we manage threatening objects? *Cogn. Process.* 13 (Suppl. 1): S131–S513.

61. Sambo, C.F., and Iannetti, G.D. (2013). Better safe than sorry? The safety margin surrounding the body is increased by anxiety. *J. Neurosci.* 33: 14225–14230.

62. Bufacchi, R.J., Liang, M., Griffin, L.D., and Iannetti, G.D. (2016). A geometric model of defensive peripersonal space. *J. Neurophysiol.* 115: 218–225.

63. Fossataro, C., Sambo, C.F., Garbarini, F., and Iannetti, G.D. (2016). Interpersonal interactions and empathy modulate perception of

threat and defensive responses. *Sci. Rep.* 6: 19353. doi: 10.1038/srep19353

64. Tipper, S.P., Lortie, C., and Bavlis, G.C. (1992). Selective reaching: evidence for action-centered attention. *J. Exp. Psychol. Hum. Percept. Perform.* 18: 891–905.

65. Griffiths, D., and Tipper, S.P. (2009). Priming of reach trajectory when observing actions: hand-centred effects. *Q. J. Exp. Psychol. (Hove)* 62: 2450–2470.

66. de Haan, A.M., Van der Stigchel, S., Nijnens, C.M., and Dijkerman, H.C. (2014). The influence of object identity on obstacle avoidance reaching behaviour. *Acta Psychol. (Amst.)* 150: 94–99.

67. Head, H., and Holmes, H.G. (1911). Sensory disturbances from cerebral lesions. *Brain* 34: 102–254.

68. Graziano, M.S.A., and Botvinick, M.M. (2002). How the brain represents the body: insights from neurophysiology and psychology. In: *Common Mechanisms in Perception and Action: Attention and Performance XIX*. Edited by W. Prinz and B. Hommel. Oxford, UK: Oxford University Press, pp. 136–157.

69. Holmes, N.P., and Spence, C. (2004). The body schema and the multisensory representation(s) of peripersonal space. *Cogn. Process.* 5: 94–105.

70. Cardinali, L., Brozzoli, C., and Farnè, A. (2009). Peripersonal space and body schema: two labels for the same concept? *Brain Topogr.* 21: 252–260.

71. Medina, J., and Coslett, H.B. (2010). From maps to form to space: touch and the body schema. *Neuropsychologia* 48: 645–654.

72. Botvinick, M., and Cohen, J. (1998). Rubber hands 'feel' touch that eyes see. *Nature* 391: 756.

73. Armel, K.C., and Ramachandran, V.S. (2003). Projecting sensations to external objects: evidence from skin conductance response. *Proc. Biol. Sci.* 270: 1499–1506.

74. Ehrsson, H.H., Spence, C., and Passingham, R.E. (2004). That's my hand! Activity in premotor cortex reflects feeling of ownership of a limb. *Science* 305: 875–877.

75. Ehrsson, H.H., Holmes, N.P., and Passingham, R.E. (2005). Touching a rubber hand: feeling of body ownership is associated with activity in multisensory brain areas. *J. Neurosci.* 25: 10564–10573.

76. Ehrsson, H.H., Wiech, K., Weiskopf, N., Dolan, R.J., and Passingham, R.E. (2007). Threatening a rubber hand that you feel is yours elicits a cortical anxiety response. *Proc. Natl. Acad. Sci. U.S.A.* 104: 9828–9833.

77. Slater, M., Perez-Marcos, D., Ehrsson, H.H., and Sanchez-Vives, M.V. (2009). Inducing illusory ownership of a virtual body. *Front. Neurosci.* 3: 214–220.

78. Petkova, V.I., Björnsdotter, M., Gentile, G., Jonsson, T., Li, T.Q., and Ehrsson, H.H. (2011). From part- to whole-body ownership in the multisensory brain. *Curr. Biol.* 21: 1118–1122.

79. van der Hoort, B., Guterstam, A., and Ehrsson, H.H. (2011). Being Barbie: the size of one's own body determines the perceived size of the world. *PLoS One* 6: e20195. doi: 10.1371/journal.pone.0020195

80. van der Hoort, B., and Ehrsson H.H. (2014). Body ownership affects visual perception of object size by rescaling the visual representation of external space. *Atten. Percept. Psychophys.* 76: 1414–1428.

81. Guterstam, A., Zeberg, H., Özçiftci, V.M., and Ehrsson, H.H. (2016). The magnetic touch illusion: a perceptual correlate of visuo-tactile integration in peripersonal space. *Cognition* 155: 44–56.

82. Bremmer, F., Schlack, A., Shah, N.J., Zafiris, O., Kubischik, M., Hoffmann, K., Zilles, K., and Fink, G. R. (2001). Polymodal motion processing in posterior parietal and premotor cortex: a human fMRI study strongly implies equivalencies between humans and monkeys. *Neuron* 29: 287–296.

83. Lloyd, D., Morrison, I., and Roberts, N. (2006). Role for human posterior parietal cortex in visual processing of aversive objects in peripersonal space. *J. Neurophysiol.* 95: 205–214.

84. Makin, T.R., Holmes, N.P., and Zohary, E. (2007). Is that near my hand? Multisensory representation of peripersonal space in human intraparietal sulcus. *J. Neurosci.* 27: 731–740.

85. Makin, T. R., Holmes, N. P., Brozzoli, C., Rossetti, Y., and Farnè, A. (2009). Coding of visual space during motor preparation: approaching objects rapidly modulate corticospinal excitability in hand-centered coordinates. *J. Neurosci.* 29: 11841–11851.

86. Avenanti, A., Annela, L., and Serino, A. (2012). Suppression of premotor cortex disrupts motor coding of peripersonal space. *Neuroimage* 63: 281–288.

87. Brozzoli, C., Gentile, G., and Ehrsson, H.H. (2012). That's near my hand! Parietal and premotor coding of hand-centered space contributes to localization and self-attribution of the hand. *J. Neurosci.* 32: 14573–14582.

88. Huang, R.S., Chen, C.F., Tran, A.T., Holstein, K.L., and Sereno, M.I. (2012). Mapping multisensory parietal face and body areas in humans. *Proc. Natl. Acad. Sci. U.S.A.* 109: 18114–18119.

89. Brozzoli, C., Gentile, G., Bergouignan, L., and Ehrsson, H.H. (2013). A shared representation of the space near one-self and others in the human premotor cortex. *Curr. Biol.* 23: 1764–1768.

90. Holt, D.J., Cassidy, B.S., Yue, X., Rauch, S.L., Boeke, E.A., Nasr, S., Tootell, R.B., and Coombs, G., 3rd. (2014). Neural correlates of personal space intrusion. *J. Neurosci.* 34: 4123–4134.

91. Ferri, F., Costantini, M., Huang, Z., Perrucci, M.G., Ferretti, A., Romani, G.L., and Northoff, G. (2015). Intertrial variability in the premotor cortex accounts for individual differences in peripersonal space. *J. Neurosci.* 35: 16328–16339.

92. Holt, D.J., Boeke, E.A., Coombs, G. 3rd, DeCross, S.N., Cassidy, B.S., Stufflebeam, S., Rauch, S.L., and Tootell, R.B. (2015). Abnormalities in personal space and parietal-frontal function in schizophrenia. *Neuroimage Clin.* 9: 233–243.

Chapter 10

1. Whittaker, J.C. (1994). *Flintknapping: Making and Understanding Stone Tools.* Austin, TX: University of Texas Press.

2. Semaw, S., Rogers, M.J., Quade, J., Renne, P.R., Butler, R.F., Dominguez-Rodrigo, M., Stout, D., Hart, W.S., Pickering, T., and Simpson, S.W. (2003). 2.6-million-year-old stone tools and associated bones from OGS-6 and OGS-7, Gona, Afar, Ethiopia. *J. Hum. Evol.* 45: 169–177.

3. Stout, D. (2011). Stone tool making and the evolution of human culture and cognition. *Phil. Trans. R. Soc. B* 366: 1050–1059.

4. Whiten, A. (2015). Experimental studies illuminate the cultural transmission of percussive technologies in Homo and Pan. *Phil. Trans. R. Soc. Lond. B Biol. Sci.* 370: 20140359.

5. Iriki, A., Tanaka, M., and Iwamura, Y. (1996). Coding of modified body schema during tool use by macaque postcentral neurones. *Neuroreport* 7: 2325–2330.

6. Maravita, A., and Iriki, A. (2004). Tools for the body (schema). *Trends Cogn. Sci.* 8: 79–86.

7. Mannu, M., and Ottoni, E.B. (2009). The enhanced tool-kit of two groups of wild bearded capuchin monkeys in the Caatinga: tool making, associative use, and secondary tools. *Am. J. Primatol.* 71: 242–251.

8. Spagnoletti, N., Visalberghi, E., Ottoni, E.B., Izar, P., and Fragaszy, D.M. (2011). Stone tool use by adult wild bearded capuchin monkeys (*Cebus libidinosus*). Frequency, efficiency and tool selectivity. *J. Hum. Evol.* 61: 97–107.

9. Halligan, P.W, and Marshall, J.C. (1991). Left neglect for near but not far space in man. *Nature* 350: 498–500.

10. Berti, A., and Frassinetti, F. (2000). When far becomes near: remapping of space by tool use. *J. Cogn. Neurosci.* 12: 415–420.

11. Berti, A., Smania, N., and Allport, A. (2001). Coding of far and near space in neglect patients. *Neuroimage* 14: S98–S102.

12. Pegna, A.J., Petit, L., Caldara-Schnetzer, A.S., Khateb, A., Annoni, J.M., Sztajzel, R., and Landis, T. (2001). So near yet so far: neglect in far or near space depends on tool use. *Ann. Neurol.* 50: 820–822.

13. Longo, M.R., and Lourenco, S.F. (2006). On the nature of near space: effects of tool use and the transition to far space. *Neuropsychologia* 44: 977–981.

14. Gamberini, L., Seraglia, B., and Priftis, K. (2008). Processing of peripersonal and extrapersonal space using tools: evidence from visual line bisection in real and virtual environments. *Neuropsychologia* 46: 1298–1304.

15. Farnè, A., and Làdavas, E. (2000). Dynamic size-change of hand peripersonal space following tool use. *Neuroreport* 11: 1645–1649.

16. Maravita, A., Spence, C., Kennett, S., and Driver, J. (2002). Tool-use changes multimodal spatial interactions between vision and touch in normal humans. *Cognition* 83: B25–B34.

17. Bonifazi, S., Farnè, A., Rinaldesi, L., and Làdavas, E. (2007). Dynamic size-change of peri-hand space through tool-use: spatial extension or shift of the multi-sensory area. *J. Neuropsychol.* 1: 101–114.

18. Farnè, A., Serino, A., and Làdavas, E. (2007). Dynamic size-change of peri-hand space following tool-use: determinants and spatial characteristics revealed through cross-modal extinction. *Cortex* 43: 436–443.

19. Serino, A., Bassolino, M., Farnè, A., and Làdavas, E. (2007). Extended multisensory space in blind cane users. *Psychol. Sci.* 18: 642–648.

20. Magosso, E., Ursino, M., di Pellegrino, G., Làdavas, E., and Serino, A. (2010). Neural bases of peri-hand space plasticity through tool-use: insights from a combined computational-experimental approach. *Neuropsychologia* 48: 812–830.

21. van Elk, M., and Blanke, O. (2011). Manipulable objects facilitate cross-modal integration in peripersonal space. *PLoS One* 6: e24641. doi: 10.1371/journal.pone.0024641

22. Seraglia, B., Priftis, K., Cutini, S., and Gamberini, L. (2012). How tool use and arm position affect peripersonal space representation. *Cogn. Process.* 13 (Suppl. 1): S325–S328.

23. Canzoneri, E., Ubaldi, S., Rastelli, V., Finisguerra, A., Bassolino, M., and Serino, A. (2013). Tool-use reshapes the boundaries of body and peripersonal space representations. *Exp. Brain Res.* 228: 25–42.

24. Bourgeois, J., Farnè, A., and Coello, Y. (2014). Costs and benefits of tool-use on the perception of reachable space. *Acta Psychol. (Amst.)* 148: 91–95.

25. Serino, A., Canzoneri, E., Marzolla, M., di Pellegrino, G., and Magosso, E. (2015). Extending peripersonal space representation without tool-use: evidence from a combined behavioral-computational approach. *Front. Behav. Neurosci.* 9: 4. doi: 10.3389/fnbeh.2015.00004

26. Galli, G., Noel, J.P., Canzoneri, E., Blanke, O., and Serino, A. (2015). The wheelchair as a full-body tool extending the peripersonal space. *Front. Psychol.* 6: 639. doi: 10.3389/fpsyg.2015.00639

27. Maravita, A., Spence, C., Kennett, S., and Driver, J. (2002). Tool-use changes multimodal spatial interactions between vision and touch in normal humans. *Cognition* 83: B25–B34.

28. Holmes, N.P., Calvert, G.A., and Spence, C. (2004). Extending or projecting peripersonal space with tools? Multisensory interactions highlight only the distal and proximal ends of tools. *Neurosci. Lett.* 372: 62–67.

29. Holmes, N.P., Sanabria, D., Calvert, G.A., and Spence, C. (2007). Tool-use: capturing multisensory spatial attention or extending multisensory peripersonal space? *Cortex* 43: 469–489.

30. Holmes, N.P. (2012). Does tool use extend peripersonal space? A review and re-analysis. *Exp. Brain Res.* 218: 273–282.

31. Luppino, G., Murata, A., Govoni, P., and Matelli, M. (1999). Largely segregated parietofrontal connections linking rostral intraparietal cortex (areas AIP and VIP) and the ventral premotor cortex (areas F5 and F4). *Exp. Brain Res.* 128: 181–187.
32. Alstermark, B., and Isa, T. (2012). Circuits for skilled reaching and grasping. *Annu. Rev. Neurosci.* 35: 559–578.
33. Konen, C.S., Mruczek, R.E., Montoya, J.L., and Kastner, S. (2013). Functional organization of human posterior parietal cortex: grasping- and reaching-related activations relative to topographically organized cortex. *J. Neurophysiol.* 109: 2897–9208.
34. Caminiti, R., Ferraina, S., and Johnson, P.B. (1996). The sources of visual information to the primate frontal lobe: a novel role for the superior parietal lobule. *Cereb. Cortex* 6: 319–328.
35. Chao, L.L., and Martin, A. (2000). Representation of manipulable man-made objects in the dorsal stream. *Neuroimage* 12: 478–484.
36. Lewis, J.W. (2006). Cortical networks related to human use of tools. *The Neuroscientist* 12: 211–231.
37. Valyear, K.F., Cavina-Pratesi, C., Stiglick, A.J., and Culham, J.C. (2007). Does tool-related fMRI activity within the intraparietal sulcus reflect the plan to grasp? *Neuroimage* 36 (Suppl. 2): T94–T108.
38. Chouinard, P.A., and Goodale, M.A. (2012). FMRI-adaptation to highly-rendered color photographs of animals and manipulable artifacts during a classification task. *Neuroimage* 59: 2941–2951.
39. Mruczek, R.E., von Loga, I.S., and Kastner, S. (2013). The representation of tool and non-tool object information in the human intraparietal sulcus. *J. Neurophysiol.* 109: 2883–2896.

Chapter 11

1. Cooke, D.F., and Graziano, M.S.A. (2004). Super-flinchers and nerves of steel: defensive movements altered by chemical manipulation of a cortical motor area. *Neuron* 43: 585–593.
2. Stoker, B. (1897). *Dracula.* London, UK: Archibald Constable and Co.
3. James, E.L. (2011). *Fifty Shades of Grey.* New York: Vintage Books.
4. Griffiths, D., and Tipper, S.P. (2009). Priming of reach trajectory when observing actions: hand-centred effects. *Q. J. Exp. Psychol. (Hove)* 62: 2450–2470.

5. Heed, T., Habets, B., Sebanz, N., and Knoblich, G. (2010). Others' actions reduce crossmodal integration in peripersonal space. *Curr. Biol.* 20: 1345–1349.

6. Brozzoli, C., Gentile, G., Bergouignan, L., and Ehrsson, H.H. (2013). A shared representation of the space near oneself and others in the human premotor cortex. *Curr. Biol.* 23: 1764–1768.

7. Teneggi, C., Canzoneri, E., di Pellegrino, G., and Serino, A. (2013). Social modulation of peripersonal space boundaries. *Curr. Biol.* 23: 406–411.

8. Fini, C., Costantini, M., and Committeri, G. (2014). Sharing space: the presence of other bodies extends the space judged as near. *PLoS One* 9: e114719. doi: 10.1371/journal.pone.0114719

9. Holt, D.J., Cassidy, B.S., Yue, X., Rauch, S.L., Boeke, E.A., Nasr, S., Tootell, R.B., and Coombs, G., 3rd. (2014). Neural correlates of personal space intrusion. *J. Neurosci.* 34: 4123–4134.

10. Iachini, T., Coello, Y., Frassinetti, F., and Ruggiero, G. (2014). Body space in social interactions: a comparison of reaching and comfort distance in immersive virtual reality. *PLoS One* 9: e111511. doi: 10.1371/journal.pone.0111511

11. Cléry, J., Guipponi, O., Wardak, C., and Ben Hamed, S. (2015). Neuronal bases of peripersonal and extrapersonal spaces, their plasticity and their dynamics: knowns and unknowns. *Neuropsychologia* 70: 313–326.

12. Holt, D.J., Boeke, E.A., Coombs, G., 3rd, DeCross, S.N., Cassidy, B.S., Stufflebeam, S., Rauch, S.L., and Tootell, R.B. (2015). Abnormalities in personal space and parietal-frontal function in schizophrenia. *Neuroimage Clin.* 9: 233–243.

13. Maister, L., Cardini, F., Zamariola, G., Serino, A., and Tsakiris, M. (2015). Your place or mine: shared sensory experiences elicit a remapping of peripersonal space. *Neuropsychologia* 70: 455–461.

14. Fossataro, C., Sambo, C.F., Garbarini, F., and Iannetti, G.D. (2016). Interpersonal interactions and empathy modulate perception of threat and defensive responses. *Sci. Rep.* 6: 19353. doi: 10.1038/srep19353

15. Quesque, F., Ruggiero, G., Mouta, S., Santos, J., Iachini, T., and Coello, Y. (2016). Keeping you at arm's length: modifying peripersonal space influences interpersonal distance. *Psychol. Res.* doi: 10.1007/s00426-016-0782-1

Chapter 12

1. von Hooff, J.A.R.A.M. (1962). Facial expression in higher primates. *Symp. Zool. Soc. Lond.* 8: 97–125.
2. von Hooff, J.A.R.A.M. (1972). A comparative approach to the phylogeny of laughter and smiling. In: *Non Verbal Communication.* Edited by R.A. Hind. Cambridge, U.K.: Cambridge University Press, pp. 209–241.
3. Thierry, B., Demaria, C., Preuschoft, S., and Desportes, C. (1989). Structural convergence between silent bared-teeth display and relaxed open-mouth display in the Tonkean macaque (*Macaca tonkeana*). *Folia Primatol. (Basel)* 52: 178–184.
4. Preuschoft, S. (1992). "Laughter" and "smile" in Barbary macaques (*Macaca sylvanus*). *Ethology* 91: 220–236.
5. De Marco, A., and Visalberghi, E. (2007). Facial displays in young tufted Capuchin monkeys (*Cebus apella*): appearance, meaning, context and target. *Folia Primatol. (Basel)* 78: 118–137.
6. Beisner, B.A., and McCowan, B. (2014). Signaling context modulates social function of silent bared-teeth displays in rhesus macaques (*Macaca mulatta*). *Am. J Primatol.* 76: 111–121.
7. Duchenne G.-B. (1990). *The Mechanism of Human Facial Expression.* Edited and translated by R. Andrew Cuthbertson. New York: Cambridge University Press. [Originally published in 1862.]
8. Darwin, C. (1872). *The Expression of the Emotions in Man and Animals.* London: John Murray.
9. Dawkins, R., and Krebs, J.R. (1978). Animal signals: information or manipulation? In: *Behavioral Ecology: An Evolutionary Approach.* Edited by R. Krebs and N.B. Davies. Oxford, U.K.: Blackwell, pp. 282–309.
10. Grafen, A., and Johnstone, R.A. (1993). Why we need ESS signalling theory. *Phil. Trans. R. Soc. Lond. (Biol.)* 340: 245–250.
11. Fridlund, A. (1994). *Human Facial Expression: An Evolutionary View.* New York: Academic Press.
12. Godfray, H.C.J., and Johnstone, R.A. (2000). Begging and bleating: the evolution of parent-offspring signaling. *Phil. Trans. R. Soc. Lond. (Biol.)* 355: 1581–1591.
13. Schmidt, K.L., and Cohn, J.F. (2001). Human facial expressions as adaptations: evolutionary questions in facial expression research. *Am. J. Phys. Anthropol.* Suppl. 33: 3–24.

Chapter 13

1. Darwin, C. (1872). *The Expression of the Emotions in Man and Animals*. London: John Murray.
2. von Hooff, J.A.R.A.M. (1962). Facial expression in higher primates. *Symp. Zool. Soc. Lond.* 8: 97–125.
3. Jolly, A. (1966). *Lemur Behaviour: A Madagascar Field Study*. Chicago: University of Chicago Press.
4. von Hooff, J.A.R.A.M. (1972). A comparative approach to the phylogeny of laughter and smiling. In: *Non Verbal Communication*. Edited by R.A. Hind. Cambridge, U.K.: Cambridge University Press, pp. 209–241.
5. Henry, J.D., and Herrero, S.M. (1974). Social play in the American black bear: its similarity to canid social play and an examination of its identifying characteristics. *Am Zoologist* 14: 371–389.
6. Preuschoft, S. (1992). "Laughter" and "smile" in Barbary macaques (*Macaca sylvanus*). *Ethology* 91: 220–236.
7. von Hooff, J.A.R.A.M., and Preuscholft, S. (2003). Laughter and smiling: the intertwining of nature and culture. In: *Animal Social Complexity*. Edited by F.B.M. de Waal and P.L. Tyack. Cambridge, MA: Harvard University Press, pp. 260–287.
8. Palagi, E. (2006). Social play in bonobos (*Pan paniscus*) and chimpanzees (*Pan troglodytes*): implications for natural social systems and interindividual relationships. *Am. J. Phys. Anthropol.* 129: 418–426.
9. Palagi, E. (2008). Sharing the motivation to play: the use of signals in adult bonobos. *Animal Behav.* 75: 887–896.
10. Palagi, E. (2009). Adult play fighting and potential role of tail signals in ring-tailed lemurs (*Lemur catta*). *J. Comp. Psychol.* 123: 1–9.
11. Ross, M.D., Owren, M.J., and Zimmermann, E. (2010). The evolution of laughter in great apes and humans. *Commun. Integr. Biol.* 3: 191–194.
12. Palagi, E., Norscia, I., and Spada, G. (2014). Relaxed open mouth as a playful signal in wild ring-tailed lemurs. *Am. J. Primatol.* 76: 1074–1083.
13. Cordoni, G., Nicotra, V., and Palagi, E. (2016). Unveiling the "secret" of play in dogs (*Canis lupus familiaris*): asymmetry and signals. *J. Comp. Psychol.* 130: 278–287.
14. Graziano, M.S.A. (2008). *The Intelligent Movement Machine*. New York: Oxford University Press.

15. Provine, R.R. (2001). *Laughter: A Scientific Investigation.* New York: Penguin.

Chapter 14

1. Ekman, P., and Friesen, W.V. (1972). *Emotion in the Human Face: Guidelines for Research and an Integration of Findings.* Oxford, UK: Pergamon Press.
2. Darwin, C. (1872). *The Expression of the Emotions in Man and Animals.* London: John Murray.
3. Andrew, R.J. (1963). The origin and evolution of the calls and facial expressions of the primates. *Behaviour* 20: 1–107.
4. Morgan, M.H., and Carrier, D.R. (2013). Protective buttressing of the human fist and the evolution of hominin hands. *J. Exp. Biol.* 216: 236–244.
5. Carrier D., and Morgan, M. (2014). Protective buttressing of the hominin face. *Biol. Rev. Camb. Philos. Soc.* 90: 330–346.

Chapter 15

1. Portwood, M. (2014). *Developmental Dyspraxia: Identification and Intervention: A Manual for Parents and Professionals.* New York: Routledge.
2. Ribolsi, M., Di Lorenzo, G., Lisi, G., Niolu, C., and Siracusano, A. (2015). A critical review and meta-analysis of the perceptual pseudoneglect across psychiatric disorders: is there a continuum? *Cogn. Process.* 16: 17–25.
3. Halligan, P.W, and Marshall, J.C. (1991). Left neglect for near but not far space in man. *Nature* 350: 498–500.
4. Rettew, D.C., and Pawlowski, S. (2016). Bullying. *Child Adolesc. Psychiatr. Clin. N. Am.* 25: 235–242.
5. Rogers, J.H. (1980). Romberg and his test. *J. Laryngol. Otol.* 94: 1401–1404.
6. Ferrè, E.R., and Haggard, P. (2016). The vestibular body: vestibular contributions to bodily representations. *Cogn. Neuropsychol.* 33: 67–81.
7. Pfeiffer, C., Serino, A., and Blanke, O. (2014). The vestibular system: a spatial reference for bodily self-consciousness. *Front. Integr. Neurosci.* 8: 31. doi: 10.3389/fnint.2014.00031

8. Bremmer, F., Klam, F., Duhamel, J.R., Ben Hamed, S., and Graf, W. (2002). Visual-vestibular interactive responses in the macaque ventral intraparietal area (VIP). *Eur. J. Neurosci.* 16: 1569–1586.
9. Gabel, S.F., Misslisch, H., Gielen, C.C., and Duysens, J. (2002). Responses of neurons in area VIP to self-induced and external visual motion. *Exp. Brain Res.* 147: 520–528.
10. Fregly, A.R., Bergstedt, M., and Graybiel, A. (1967). Relationships between blood alcohol, positional alcohol nystagmus and postural equilibrium. *Q. J. Stud. Alcohol* 28: 11–21.

Index

Note: Page numbers followed by an italicized "*f*" indicate figures.